WORD
AND SPIRIT

Text copyright © Will Donaldson 2011
The author asserts the moral right
to be identified as the author of this work

Published by
The Bible Reading Fellowship
15 The Chambers, Vineyard
Abingdon OX14 3FE
United Kingdom
Tel: +44 (0)1865 319700
Email: enquiries@brf.org.uk
Website: www.brf.org.uk
BRF is a Registered Charity
I
SBN 978 1 84101 825 6
First published 2011
10 9 8 7 6 5 4 3 2 1 0

Acknowledgments
Unless otherwise stated, scripture quotations are taken from the Holy Bible, New International
Version, copyright © 1973, 1978, 1984 by International Bible Society, and are used by
permission of Hodder & Stoughton Publishers, a member of the Hachette Livre UK Group.
All rights reserved. 'NIV' is a registered trademark of International Bible Society. UK trademark
number 1448790.

Scripture quotations taken from The Holy Bible, Today's New International Version. Copyright
© 2004 by International Bible Society. Used by permission of Hodder & Stoughton
Publishers, a member of the Hachette Livre UK Group. All rights reserved.

Scripture quotations taken from The Revised Standard Version of the Bible, copyright © 1946,
1952, 1971 by the Division of Christian Education of the National Council of the Churches of
Christ in the United States of America, are used by permission. All rghts reserved.

New King James Version of the Bible copyright © 1979, 1980, 1982 by Thomas Nelson, Inc.
All rights reserved.

New English Bible copyright © 1961, 1970 by Oxford University Press and Cambridge
University Press.

* Adm. by worshiptogether.com songs excl. UK & Europe, adm. by kingswaysongs.com
tym@kingsway.co.uk. Used by permission.

Extracts from the service for the Ordination of Deacons, *Common Worship*, copyright © The
Archbishop's Council. Used by permission.

A catalogue record for this book is available from the British Library

Printed in Singapore by Craft Print International Ltd

WORD
AND SPIRIT

THE VITAL PARTNERSHIP IN
CHRISTIAN LEADERSHIP

WILL DONALDSON

FOREWORD

Two things appear crystal clear to me. The first is that throughout the journey of God's dealings with humankind, as recorded in the Bible, God consistently worked through *both* his proclaimed Word *and* through his demonstrated Spirit's power; the second is that today's church has largely opted for an 'either/or': seeking God's manifest power *or* studying and proclaiming his Word. Must we decide? Must we divide? Must we chose 'either/or'? Cannot we have 'both–and'?

Will Donaldson boldly and biblically declares 'Both'. In his wonderful new book *Word and Spirit*, he distils decades of walking close to God in faithful ministry, and his conclusion is that the biblical Christian will rely on the Spirit's power, and the truly Charismatic believer will be led by that Spirit to rely on God's Word. Will demonstrates convincingly from a sustained study of Scripture and Tradition that Tertullian was correct to claim, 'The two hands of God are Word and Spirit.'

The book's tone is irenic: Will is a reconciler. He wants to bring together two brothers often in dispute, two communities and traditions that have often point-scored, or been suspicious of or separated from one another. What makes this book so unique, and so special, is that it is written by someone who has understood both 'camps', deeply listened to both, truly benefited from both, and truly loves both. Indeed, Will Donaldson is one of those rare Christians who embodies this message. I am thrilled to be able to commend this book and pray that it will equip its readers to imitate the Saviour 'powerful in word and deed' (Luke 24:19).

Simon Ponsonby
Pastor of Theology, St Aldates, Oxford
Dean of Studies, Oxford Centre of Church Growth

CONTENTS

✜

INTRODUCTION

Our gospel came to you not simply with words, but also with power, with the Holy Spirit and with deep conviction... You welcomed the message with the joy given by the Holy Spirit.

1 Thessalonians 1:5–6

When I was eleven years old, I went on a school skiing trip to Aviemore in Scotland. I wasn't the world's greatest skier but, by the end of the week, I was getting the hang of it. The secret was to keep the two skis in a harmonious partnership: moving them in alternate strides when travelling along the level, holding them in exact parallel when gliding downhill, and forming an arrowhead with them when needing to slow down and stop. It required great concentration on both skis all the time: it was both exhausting and exhilarating.

My experience of Christian ministry has been of a similar harmonious partnership. Having been brought up in a churchgoing family, I was introduced to Jesus at the age of 13 at a Christian houseparty in Dorset one summer. As I came to know and love Jesus as my friend and Saviour, I also came to love the Bible. I loved to hear it explained in the talks, enjoyed studying it in small groups and devoured it in my own personal quiet times. I was also very aware that the Holy Spirit had taken up residence in my life, teaching me from the Bible, changing me to be like Jesus and strengthening me to serve him at school and at home.

During my time at university in Cambridge, reading History (1975–78), I became aware of a growing vocation to ordination in the Church of England. When selected for training, I returned to Cambridge for three more years to study theology and train for full-time ministry at Ridley Hall (1979–82). Throughout these six years, I was fully involved in the university Christian Union and valued getting to know Christians across the evangelical spectrum, drawn together by our common love for Jesus and his Word. I was aware that the local churches in Cambridge had different flavours (theologically), but the Christian Union seemed to draw us together in a glorious unity. Although I was at the more 'Conservative' end of the spectrum at this stage (in theological terms), I respected and admired those who were at the more 'Charismatic' end. They were my close friends and companions in serving Jesus, and I loved their openness to and dependency on the Holy Spirit.

I married into a strong Christian family and discovered that two of my ordained brothers-in-law were at the more Charismatic end of the spectrum. They were a number of years my senior, so I listened and learned from them about ministry in the power of the Spirit and the use of spiritual gifts. But I was aware of the need to hold my theology together in a harmonious partnership: during my two curacies I benefited greatly by attending the Fairmile Preaching Conferences organised by the church of St Helen's, Bishopsgate, and I learnt the priority and skills of expository preaching. It has remained my priority throughout 25 years of parish ministry.

During my first curacy in inner-city Liverpool, I received a superb all-round training in parish ministry under the prayerful and godly supervision of my training incumbent, Malcolm Dean. It was during my second curacy at St Mary's, Reigate, that I came into a personal experience of Charismatic renewal. It was not wildly dramatic but it was hugely significant. My vicar, Richard Thompson, was a committed evangelical and was also open to the Spirit's ministry of renewal. He invited a team from St Andrew's, Chorleywood, to come over for an evening of worship, teaching and ministry. By this stage, I had read or listened to leading Charismatic evangelicals such as David Watson, Michael Green, David Prior, George Carey, Michael Harper and David Pawson, and now the time seemed right for me to get out of the shallow end into the deeper waters of the Spirit. I went forward for prayer during the ministry time at the end of the meeting and felt an amazing experience of being known and loved by God. I found myself praising God in a new and unknown tongue, and felt a fresh wave of God's power and strength for my ministry.

I believe it was God's way of preparing me for what lay ahead: within a year I had been appointed to be vicar of a challenging inner-city parish in Bristol (the Easton Christian Family Centre). It was characterised by urban poverty, high crime rates, broken families and homelessness, as well as large minorities of Hindus, Sikhs and Muslims. Having a strong, lively congregation, we sensed God's renewed call to share the gospel with the local community and developed a ten-year mission plan for the Decade of Evangelism (1990–99). I was also increasingly aware of God's empowering presence: his Holy Spirit equipping us to bring God's healing grace to this broken community. It was the harmonious partnership again: the Word of God and the Spirit of God working together for the glory of God. We desperately needed both.

After nearly ten years it was time for us to move, and God called us to West London and the parish of St John with St James, Ealing. It was a larger church with many more professionals, but with a real social mix in the congregation, too. They were hungry for Bible teaching, pastoral care and, above all, a real experience of God. Here the harmonious partnership of Word and Spirit emerged again: I majored on discipleship, expository preaching and evangelism but also created opportunities for the Spirit to work through worship, prayer ministry and spiritual gifts. God did a gracious work of rebuilding his people and drawing in others to discover him through the ministry of the church. I became more convinced than ever of the vital partnership between the Scriptures and the Spirit. It was especially evident in our two 'fresh expressions of church' ('Café Church' for the homeless and 'the Maze' for teenagers). Both of these groups needed to *experience* God's love, not just know about it from sermons and talks. It was during these years that we became regular attendees at the New Wine summer conferences with many from our church, and the ongoing impact was tangible over that time. It provided an exciting combination of lively worship, careful Bible teaching, prayer ministry and wonderful fellowship. I came back each year with fresh vision and renewed power. But I also valued my ongoing links with more Conservative evangelicals through the Diocesan Evangelical Fellowship and the London Men's Convention, and I continued to hold the evangelical priorities of expository preaching and evangelism nearest to my heart.

God brought us to Oxford in September 2007, when I was appointed Director of Christian Leadership at Wycliffe Hall. Not only were there students from all shades of evangelical churches, but I discovered that training Christian leaders was a partnership of Word and Spirit, too. Students study the Bible and grow in theological wisdom and knowledge, but they also let the Spirit of God transform them more fully into the image of his Son and equip them with power and gifts for Christian ministry.

This book is written in the deep conviction that the Word and the Spirit are God's two greatest resources for Christian leadership and that godly leadership requires us to sit humbly under the authority of both.[1] They need to be kept in partnership at all times, and gospel ministry must allow them to do their work of drawing people to Christ, growing churches and transforming society. I hope this book will challenge Christian leaders who love to teach the Bible to be more open to the full breath of the Spirit's work (as the Bible defines it), and those who love the Spirit's ministry in that fuller breath to make Bible teaching their greatest priority (as the Bible requires it).[2] I am aware that this will have a particular relevance to the Evangelical constituency, but I sincerely hope that there will be a wider reading by people of any persuasion who want to think through issues of authentic Christian theology and practice. I pray that this book will help you.

What, then, are the key tasks of Christian leadership in a local church, and how do Word and Spirit resource these ministries? My answer is set out in Chapters 4 to 10, covering the areas of preaching and teaching the Bible, developing and implementing vision, working in teams and mentoring future leaders, mobilising every member into ministry, enabling worship and prayer, providing pastoral care and nurture, and motivating evangelism and mission. I have chosen these areas for four reasons: first, I think the Bible identifies them as the primary tasks for a local church leader; second, I believe they reflect the priorities of some of the greatest Christian leaders in the history of the Church; third, they reflect the best wisdom from the current Christian literature on church leadership; and fourth, they express my considered reflections after 25 years of trying to get it right. In other words, if I had my time over again, these are the seven areas I would concentrate on. While they are not the only tasks that God might expect of us, I want to argue that they are the *main* ones. But first we will look at contemporary considerations as to why this partnership of Word and Spirit is of vital importance, before going on to examine some biblical and historical perspectives.

Notes

1   I am aware that many Christian authors feel it appropriate to use a capital 'W' only when speaking about Jesus as 'the Word made flesh' (John 1:14), and therefore would choose not to use a capital when referring to the Bible as 'the word of God'. I understand this, but I will also be using a capital 'W' for the written Word to mark its importance as the vehicle that leads us to the living Word, Jesus.
2   I am not suggesting that all churches that emphasise 'the ministry of the Word' do not have a developed theology of the Spirit, or that all churches that emphasise 'the ministry of the Spirit' do not have a strong expository preaching ministry. In fact, many churches hold them together brilliantly. I simply want to make the case for emphasising *both*, for reasons that will soon become clear.

CONTEMPORARY
CONSIDERATIONS

THE CURRENT NEED
FOR A CLOSER PARTNERSHIP

A number of fascinating studies have explored the relationship between the Word and the Spirit. During the 1970s a group nominated by the Church of England Evangelical Council and the Fountain Trust met together over a period of 18 months to explore areas of agreement between Evangelicals of Conservative and Charismatic convictions. Distinguished leaders were present, including John Stott, David Watson, Jim Packer, Colin Buchanan, John Collins, Gavin Reid and Tom Smail. The result was a joint statement published in April 1977, which said, 'We thankfully recognise that what unites us is far greater than the matters on which some of us still disagree. We share the same evangelical faith, recognising each other as brothers in Christ and in the gospel, and we desire to remain in fellowship and to build yet stronger relationships of love and trust.'[1] But the statement went beyond this to plead for a closer theological partnership of Word and Spirit: 'Both doctrine and experience, word and Spirit, must go together, biblical doctrine testing, interpreting and controlling our experience, and experience fulfilling, incarnating and expressing our beliefs.'[2]

Dr Jim Packer, in the 1980s, wrote his biblical theology of the Spirit, reflecting on the modern Charismatic movement and arguing (rightly, in my view) that all true claims and experiences of the Spirit must have a Christ-centredness, for the Spirit's special work is to glorify Christ. He also commented on the partnership of Word and Spirit:

Those who would live under the authority of the Spirit must bow before the Word as the Spirit's textbook, while those who would live under the authority of Scripture must seek the Spirit as its interpreter. Negligence and one-sidedness either way could be ruinous, and since a proper balance in this as in other matters comes naturally to none of us, we do well to be on our guard. [3]

Donald Bridge, in 1987, wrote *Power Evangelism and the Word of God*, in which he reflected on the 'Third Wave' (John Wimber's 'signs and wonders' movement) and pleaded with the Evangelical movement not to polarise. While giving a cautious welcome to many aspects of this further development of the Charismatic movement, he argued that we must keep the Bible, the cross and the gospel at the centre of our life as a Christian community: 'What does today's Church need in a day of opportunity unprecedented this century? … live orthodoxy… a virile proclamation of the truth that is unashamedly biblical and dogmatic… lived out in a demonstration that makes hell's foundations quiver.' [4]

Donald Bloesch, one of the USA's foremost Evangelical theologians, wrote *A Theology of Word and Spirit* in 1992. It was not so much an attempt to find the common ground between Conservatives and Charismatics as a proposal for an alternative way of doing theology (in continuity with the Protestant Reformers), which asserted both the objectivity and the subjectivity of Christian faith. Faith is not just about encountering the objective revelation of biblical truth; it is also the subjective revelation of the Holy Spirit, who inspired the authors of Scripture and now reveals this truth to our hearts. 'The key to effective evangelism is the regenerating and liberating work of the Holy Spirit. It is the Spirit whose role is to convict and convince (John 16:8)… Prayer in the power of the Spirit is the necessary seedbed of the Word.' For Bloesch, however, this does not in any way negate the need for proclamation of the apostolic gospel: 'The heart of evangelism is sharing the story of Christ, the good news of how God took upon himself the sin and the shame of the human race so that all who believe in him might be saved.'[5]

David Pawson, a well-known Baptist pastor and Bible teacher, wrote *Fourth Wave: Charismatics and Evangelicals: Are They Ready to Come Together?* in 1993. He makes a strong case for cherishing the best of both worlds, both on theological and pragmatic grounds. He concludes, 'God's purpose in giving us his Spirit and the Scripture was that we might be equipped to bring the good news of salvation to a sad and sinful society that does not know why it is here or where it is going. That is why he needs a people who are both charismatic and evangelical.'[6] In the republishing of the book (under a new title) in 1998, he gave further reasons for the need for this vital partnership:

Charismatics without evangelicals become vulnerable to being 'blown here and there by every eddy of teaching' (Eph. 4:14). Evangelicals without charismatics are of equal concern... Sound doctrine does not ensure spiritual dynamic. Exegesis is no substitute for experience. The church is meant to be powerful as well as pure.[7]

Two Vineyard pastors, Rich Nathan and Ken Wilson, wrote *Empowered Evangelicals: Bringing Together the Best of the Evangelical and Charismatic Worlds* in 1997. They still saw their roots solidly in the Conservative Evangelical tradition, so they provided a biblical and historical case for integration, combining the thoughtful, biblical approach of the Evangelical tradition with the vitality of the Pentecostal-Charismatic movement. 'Can we have the best of both worlds? Can a bridge be built that brings the two worlds together? We believe it can. To us, the most exciting aspect of the marriage is the conservative evangelical's historic target—the salvation of the lost—with charismatic power to get the job done.'[8] Jim Packer warmly commends this book in his foreword:

Wilson and Nathan are both pastors, not devotees of either side but men with feet in both camps, and what they want to do is help these two sorts of Bible people to benefit from each other's insights and experience at the local church level. I applaud their venture... following their lead will be a big step forward towards the unity in truth and power that our times oblige us to seek.[9]

Larry Hart, Professor of Theology in the Graduate School of Theology and Missions in Tulsa, Oklahoma, wrote *Truth Aflame: A Balanced Theology for Evangelical and Charismatics* in 1999. It was a deliberate attempt to bridge the growing rift in the Evangelical world with a systematic theology that integrated Charismatic insights into an Evangelical framework. In the preface he writes, 'The title reflects my own spiritual heritage. *Truth* evokes images of the evangelical emphasis on the Word, objective truth, and the life of the mind. *Aflame* points to the Pentecostal-charismatic stress on the Spirit, the heart, and religious affections. In her best days, the Church always has kept "heart religion" and "head religion" in balance and integrated.'[10] Roger Olsen, a fellow Professor of Theology, praises it highly: 'No other single volume of systematic theology unites these two perspectives. It is biblical, contemporary, irenic and readable.'[11]

My final example of recent books that have tried to weld together Word and Spirit is Simon Ponsonby's *God Inside Out*. Although this sets out to be an in-depth study of the Holy Spirit, it is also an extraordinary piece of bridge-building between the Conservative and Charismatic worlds, so much so that Vaughan Roberts, Rector of St Ebbe's, Oxford, endorses it confidently:

Writing from a Charismatic perspective Simon Ponsonby maintains the main emphases of the Bible's teaching, stressing the intimate relationship of the Spirit with God's Word and his work of salvation through Christ. Many of the differences between Evangelical Christians would be kept in perspective if we all followed his example of faithful and passionate engagement with Scripture.[12]

In the light of these (and other) treatments of the partnership of Word and Spirit, why is there a need for this book now?

A STRATEGIC OPPORTUNITY

The Times Saturday Review on 2 May 2009 had a huge headline, 'Spread the Word, God is back', and the two-page article explored the extraordinary growth of Evangelicalism across the world. This growth was all the more phenomenal (the journalists thought) in view of the fact that, ever since the Enlightenment, the intellectual high priests of modernity had been predicting the death of religion. But it never happened, the article said. Instead there is a renaissance of Christian faith in the USA and Europe (some two million people have been on the Alpha Course); there have been extraordinary revivals in countries that previously enforced secularism (like Russia, where 86 per cent of the population identify themselves as Christians, and China, where there are now 80 million Christians—more than are members of the Communist party); but, most significantly, 60 per cent of the world's Christian population are in the developing world (witness the massive churches in South Korea, Nigeria and Latin America). All of this was reported in the article with the typical journalistic spin of 'breaking news' and 'Isn't this weird?'

The growth of Evangelicalism is not a sudden phenomenon. Patrick Johnstone, an expert observer of worldwide Church growth, was noticing these trends in the mid-1990s: 'Never in history has such a high percentage of the world's population been exposed to the gospel, nor the increase of evangelical Christians been so encouraging.'[13] I think I would want to add a note of caution here about triumphalistic statistics, because Evangelicals have a track record of hyping them up to make us feel better, whereas the reality behind the statistics is often sobering when you look more closely and see the nominalism and worldliness of many professing Christians.

Real growth cannot be denied, however, and this is very exciting —until we realise that evangelicalism is fairly divided. Of course, there will be shades of difference in any religious movement, but Evangelicals in particular (and Protestants in general) do not have a good track record on Christian unity. Clive Calver, the General Director of the Evangelical Alliance from 1983 to 1997, wrote from considerable experience (and pain) when he said, 'Charismatic evangelicals and their non-Charismatic counterparts have frequently been most united in their mutual suspicion of one another... the damage done to our morale has been devastating, and... seriously impaired the effectiveness of our witness.'[14] In a similar vein, John Stott wrote an impassioned plea for Evangelical unity in his gem *Evangelical Truth* at the turn of the millennium:

I continue to be profoundly grieved by our evangelical tendency to fragment. During the last half century the Evangelical movement in Britain (as elsewhere) has grown out of all recognition in numbers, church life, scholarship and leadership—but not, I think, in cohesion or national influence. People now refer to the multiple 'tribes' of evangelicalism, and like to place a qualifying adjective in front of 'evangelical'. There are many to choose from... but is this really necessary?[15]

Rob Warner, in his sociological critique of the English Evangelical movement between 1966 and 2001, observes:

The broad and evolving evangelical coalition is a complex matrix of strands in tension... we conclude that the evangelical tradition appears to be in the process of bifurcation... at the end of the period studied, pan-evangelical identity appeared severely weakened, with no grouping well placed to generate new subcultural capital and to reconstruct pan-evangelical identity: the neo-conservatives are too exclusive, the activists too implausible, and the progressives too alienated.[16]

So, it seems, there is a strange, bewildering paradox here: on the one hand, an unprecedented opportunity to share the gospel and to win the nations for Christ (presented by the enormous growth of the worldwide Evangelical movement in the last 50 years) and, on the other hand, a deeply divided movement, with little inner cohesion or central focal point. The 'tribes' of Evangelicalism multiply and grow (witness the growth of movements like Reform, New Wine, Proclamation Trust and Fulcrum) but the unity of the movement has evaporated in the joy and celebrations of our tribal gatherings.

What would Jesus say? I suspect he would ask us to listen again to the prayer he prayed on the night before he died (John 17). It is a deeply impassioned prayer for the unity (v. 23) and holiness (v. 17) of his followers, around the truth of God's word (v. 17), for the sake of our mission to the world (v. 18). So Holy Scripture and Holy Spirit are both key to this unity: the Word gives us the true self-revelation of God, the saving knowledge of Christ and the secrets of faithful Christian living; the Spirit is the agent for our sanctification, bringing to us the indwelling presence of Christ and the indwelling power for Christian living and mission. This book will unashamedly focus on both because, otherwise, a glorious opportunity (which I believe God has created) might be lost.

A PRESSING CULTURAL REASON

Most readers of this book will probably be aware that the last 60 years have witnessed a massive cultural shift from the scientific certainties of the Enlightenment era (known as modernism) into the decentralised uncertainties of the postmodern era. This is not the place for a full analysis of the changes but John Stott's summary certainly gives us the feel of this new worldview set against the old one:

In general, modernism proclaims the autonomy of human reason, especially in the cold objectivity of science, whereas postmodernism prefers the warmth of subjective experience. Modernism is committed to the quest for truth, believing that certainty is attainable; postmodernism is committed to pluralism, affirming the validity of all ideologies, and tolerance as the supreme virtue. Modernism declares the inevitability of social progress; postmodernism pricks the bubble of utopian dreams. Modernism exalts self-centred individualism; but postmodernism seeks the togetherness of community. Modernism is supremely self-confident... whereas postmodernism is humble enough to question everything, for it lacks confidence in anything.[17]

Perhaps we should expand one area of this brilliant summary: modernism believed in the big story of human progress, so that humankind, armed with the twin tools of human science and human reason, was on a metaphorical escalator, onwards and upwards towards utopia. Postmodernism, on the other hand, has rightly challenged this myth of progress, on the basis of the evidence of two World Wars in the first half of the 20th century and two totalitarian regimes—Nazism and Communism—which were founded on the myth, but has wrongly concluded that there are no 'big stories' (metanarratives) at all. This conclusion encompasses religious metanarratives, too, so monotheistic faiths like Christianity, Judaism and Islam are generally 'out of favour' from a postmodern perspective. All claims to 'absolute truth' or 'unique revelation' are viewed as highly suspicious—at best, as naïve and deluded and, at worst, as devious and controlling, a veiled bid for power.

Christian responses to postmodernism have been many and varied but generally they fall into three categories. Firstly, there are responses which have been almost entirely critical, deeply suspicious and unable to find anything that might play to our advantage.[18] Secondly, some studies have embraced postmodernism and tried to view it as positively as possible, identifying all the new possibilities and opportunities that it offers the Church.[19] Thirdly, there have been studies which have tried to hold a middle way, critical of the aspects of postmodern culture where Christian truth has been threatened or denied (pluralism, relativism and consumerism, for example), but affirming of the aspects that have exploded the modernist worldview and opened up a humbler intellectual climate and a new spiritual awareness.[20]

For our purposes, I believe that the Word and the Spirit are both desperately needed in providing us with an appropriate and balanced response to postmodernism. Over and against post-modernism's distrust of metanarratives and the concept of absolute truth, the Bible affirms that there is a big story for humankind (creation, fall, redemption and consummation), and there is definitive revelation, absolute truth and historical reality in the Scriptures, which bear witness to the unique Saviour, Jesus Christ. However, in relation to postmodernism's quest for spiritual experience, community belonging and a sense of personal identity and purpose in life, Christians affirm that the Holy Spirit gives us an authentic spiritual experience, a transforming relationship with God and a new community of brothers and sisters in Christ, where we find both our true identity and our meaning and purpose to life.

Graham Cray puts it well in his *Postmodern Culture and Youth Discipleship*, in relation to the way we disciple young people who have breathed only the air of postmodern culture and have known nothing else:

God's equipment for his church involves a vital partnership of Word and Spirit. This partnership is of extra importance in a time of cultural transition. The Word (in the sense of the Scriptures—the word about the Word) is God's living message, his gift from the past. It is the authoritative and supreme record of who our God is, what he has done, and how his people are to live. It is critical that we arm our young people with an understanding of Scripture... The Spirit is the gift of God from the future. The Spirit is the foretaste and guarantee of the future Christ has won... his calling is to enable each generation to live faithfully as a foretaste of God's coming kingdom. He did it for our own generation; we can trust him to do it for our children, however different their world may be.[21]

What was true for young people at the turn of the millennium is true for all of us now. Postmodernism is the air we all breathe and, if we are to remain faithful to God in this new cultural context, we will need both Word and Spirit to help us. Professor Robert Webber has identified 24 characteristics of the way younger evangelicals are thinking, having grown up in postmodern culture, and he talks about their having a different commitment to truth: *'Younger evangelicals are attracted to absolutes.* But they don't want to arrive at absolutes through evidence and logic... They want truth that is a matter of "heart as well as mind"... The importance of truth is not so much that it is understood but that it is loved and lived.'[22] I would argue that Christian truth does need to be understood as well as experienced, and that is why we need God's Word and God's Spirit more than ever.

A REQUIREMENT OF MINISTERIAL TRAINING

Evangelical churches have been producing the largest numbers of ordinands since the 1990s.[23] This is a tribute to the passion and commitment of their incumbents and the faith and vitality of the church communities that have nurtured and inspired these future leaders. Before coming to Wycliffe Hall, I had the privilege of being one of the Directors of Ordinands for the Willesden Area of the London Diocese (while still Vicar of St John's, Ealing) and I explored the future vocations of a dozen candidates. It was so encouraging to see the way God was calling many of them into full-time ministry, and inspiring to witness their love for Christ and their growing desire to serve him. Three of the candidates I met with ended up having me as their tutor at Wycliffe Hall!

Despite the growing polarisation within Evangelicalism between churches and movements that emphasise 'the ministry of the Word' and others that emphasise 'the ministry of the Spirit', there is an internal dynamic in ministerial training which ensures that both Word and Spirit have to be taken seriously. I will explain what

I mean and then describe how we do this at Wycliffe Hall, by way of an example.

All ministerial training colleges and courses have three key components:

- Theological education, which involves biblical studies, Church history, ecclesiology, doctrine, philosophy, ethics, comparative religions and so on.
- Ministerial training, which involves preaching, worship, pastoral care, leadership, mission, apologetics and evangelism, with practical opportunities in placements and missions to gain experience and learn the art of theological reflection.
- Spiritual formation, which focuses on the inner life—our relationship with God, our patterns of prayer, our worship, our attitudes and lifestyle, our relationships with others, our personality and character and how they shape our leadership, and the ongoing healing of our past wounds and hurts.

All three of these areas are vital in preparing men and women for their future ministries.

We should notice how Word and Spirit need to be involved in each of the three areas. Theological education is wider than studying the Bible but must never depart from it if we sit under the authority of God's written Word. A robust and confident biblical theology should inform all our theological thinking. Yet the Bible itself points us to the Spirit, who leads us into all truth[24] and illuminates our study of the Bible. Without the illumination of the Spirit, our minds are darkened and our understanding impaired.

It is similar with ministerial training: the Word of God shapes our vision of Christian ministry and especially our role as Christian leaders. How we preach and lead worship, how we mobilise pastoral care and evangelism, how we give leadership and serve the flock of God—all of these are informed by the Bible, particularly the example of Jesus, the patterns of the early Church and the teaching of the epistles. But the Spirit of God shapes our ministerial training, too (often when we are faced with real ministry experiences in placements and missions): he equips us with spiritual gifts, he anoints us with power for ministry and mission, and he gives us wisdom and understanding for the complex issues that we face in parish life.

Likewise with spiritual formation: the Word of God teaches us how to know and love God, how to conduct our personal relationships and how to understand ourselves with all our strengths and frailties. But the Spirit is our Comforter and Counsellor, helping us to know the Father and the Son, leading us in prayer, restoring damaged relationships, transforming our characters and healing our wounds.

Therefore, at Wycliffe Hall, for example, we unashamedly emphasise Word and Spirit in our training of men and women for their future ministries. Alongside the lectures in biblical studies and homiletics, the Word of God is expounded in daily worship in chapel, studied in fellowship groups and worked at in preaching classes. We also have Bible-themed days, annual preaching conferences and opportunities to do supervised preaching in local churches and on summer placements. We are eager to let the Bible shape all our thinking about and preparation for our future ministries, and we want to send out workers 'who correctly handle the word of truth' (2 Timothy 2:15). The Spirit of God, too, pervades all our training, teaching us from the Bible, being present in our times of corporate worship, equipping us in times of prayer, deepening our love for Christ and shaping us into the ministers that God has called us to be. In fact, we have a special week focusing on 'The Holy Spirit in Ministry', which explores biblical, doctrinal and historical perspectives and examines areas like spiritual gifts, healing and the Spirit's empowering for mission.

Theological colleges and ministerial training courses have a wonderful opportunity to weld together Word and Spirit in the hearts and minds of future Christian leaders. The Ordinal of the Church of England (the order of service for ordination) certainly requires those being ordained as deacons and priests to realise their dependency on and commitment to both Word and Spirit.

The Bishop says, 'Deacons are called to proclaim the gospel in word and deed... they preach the Word... they are to seek nourishment from the Scriptures; they are to study them with God's people, that the whole church may be equipped to live out the gospel in the world.'

Then he asks them, 'Do you accept the Holy Scriptures as revealing all things necessary for eternal salvation through faith in Jesus Christ?' The candidates reply, 'I do so accept them.' Then, 'Will you be diligent in prayer, in reading Holy Scripture, and in all studies that will deepen your faith and fit you to bear witness to the truth of the gospel?' And they reply, 'By the help of God I will.' In other words, we are ordained to a ministry of the Word, alongside other ministries such as leading worship, pastoral care and evangelism, and we are nourished and guided in our ministry by that same Word of God.

But this ministry is to be done in the anointing and power of the Holy Spirit. The Bishop also asks them: 'Will you then, in the strength of the Holy Spirit, continually stir up the gift of God that is in you?' And the reply is 'By the help of God, I will.' Then the Bishop says to the candidates, 'You cannot bear the weight of this calling in your own strength, but only by the grace and power of God. Pray therefore that your heart may daily be enlarged and your understanding of the Scriptures enlightened. Pray earnestly for the gift of the Holy Spirit.' The ordination prayer itself asks for each candidate to be anointed with God's Spirit: 'Send down the Holy Spirit upon your servant for the office and work of a deacon in your Church'; similarly, the following prayer requests, 'Through your Spirit, heavenly Father, give these your servants grace and power to fulfil their ministry.'

Then it is back to the Word again. The Bishop hands each candidate a New Testament, with the charge, 'Receive this book, as a sign of the authority given you this day and speak God's Word to his people. Build them up in his truth and serve them in his name.' The service ends with a trinitarian blessing that brings Word and Spirit together for one last time:

May the Father, whose glory fills the heavens, cleanse you by his holiness and send you to proclaim his Word. Amen!

May Christ, who has ascended to the heights, pour upon you the riches of his grace. Amen!

May the Holy Spirit, the comforter, equip you and strength you in your ministry. Amen!

And the blessing of God Almighty, the Father, the Son, and the Holy Spirit, be upon you and remain with you always.

CONCLUSION

To summarise, these are the three issues that lie behind this book: a desire to see unity in the evangelical movement at a time of tremendous opportunity; a pressing cultural need to allow Word and Spirit to address the challenges and opportunities of postmodernism; and the glorious opportunity given by theological colleges and ministerial courses to weld together Word and Spirit in the minds and hearts of future church leaders. However, these issues are subsidiary to deeper and more important theological ones: are Word and Spirit welded together in biblical theology, and are there any historical precedents for this vital partnership in Christian leadership? To these questions we now turn.

Notes

1   'Gospel and Spirit', published by the Fountain Trust and the Church of England Council (The Abbey Press, April 1977), p. 1

2   'Gospel and Spirit', p. 2

3   Jim Packer, *Keep in Step with the Spirit* (IVP, 1984) p. 240

4   Donald Bridge, *Power Evangelism and the Word of God* (Kingsway, 1987), p. 243

5   Donald Bloesch, *A Theology of Word and Spirit* (IVP, 1992), pp. 231–232

6   David Pawson, *Fourth Wave* (Hodder and Stoughton, 1993), p. 136

7   David Pawson, *Word and Spirit Together* (Hodder and Stoughton, 1998), p. 3

8   Rich Nathan and Ken Wilson, *Empowered Evangelicals* (Vine, 1997), p. 34

9   Nathan and Wilson, *Empowered Evangelicals*, pp. 7–8

10 Larry Hart, *Truth Aflame* (Thomas Nelson, 1999), Preface

11 Hart, *Truth Aflame*, front cover

12 Simon Ponsonby, *God Inside Out* (Kingsway, 2007), p. 1

13 Patrick Johnstone, *Operation World* (OM, 1996 edition), p. 35

14 Pawson, *Fourth Wave*, p. 7

15 John Stott, *Evangelical Truth* (IVP, 1999), p. 9

16 Rob Warner, *Reinventing English Evangelicalism 1966–2001* (Paternoster, 2007),
    p. 241

17 John Stott, *The Living Church* (IVP, 2007), p. 15

18 Douglas Groothius' *Truth Decay* (IVP, 2000) might fall into this category. It is
    a powerful and searching critique, but ends up warning Christians to have
    nothing to do with it, as if modernism was a better place to be.

19 Gerard Kelly's *Get a Grip on the Future* (Monarch, 1999) might come into
    this category, in his very clear analysis of postmodernism and his tentative
    suggestions for the church in terms of its life and witness.

20 Graham Cray's *Postmodern Culture and Youth Discipleship* (Grove, reprinted 2000)
    is a good example of this critical and positive engagement. Also *Mission-Shaped
    Church* (CHP, 2nd impression 2005), ch. 1.

21 Cray, *Postmodern Culture and Youth Discipleship*, p. 21

22 Robert Webber, *The Younger Evangelicals* (Baker, 2002), p. 52

23 Roger Steer, *Church on Fire* (Hodder, 1998), p. 424

24 I realise there is a primary meaning here which needs to be applied to the
    apostolic testimony to Jesus, now contained in the New Testament. But it is
    widely recognised that there is a secondary application to all Christians, in
    that the Holy Spirit is our teacher and the spiritual truths of the Bible need to
    be revealed, not just taught. See John Stott, *Understanding the Bible* (SU, revised
    edition 1984), p. 150.

THEOLOGICAL
FOUNDATIONS

BIBLICAL PERSPECTIVES

The Thirty-Nine Articles of Religion may not be the most widely read pieces of Anglican literature but they are, arguably, the most important. They were established in 1563 as the defining doctrinal statement of the Anglican Church and, despite their particular relevance to the historical and doctrinal debates of the 16th century, remain so today, along with the Book of Common Prayer, the Ordinal and the historic creeds.

Article 20 addresses the issue of the authority of the Church in relation to the Bible. It states that 'it is not lawful for the Church to ordain anything contrary to God's Word written, neither may it so expound one place of Scripture, that it be repugnant to another'. The reason I highlight it is because I think there has been a tendency in both Conservative and Charismatic circles to do just this: for Conservatives to expound a doctrine of Scripture that minimises the doctrine of the Spirit,[1] and for Charismatics to expound a doctrine of the Spirit that minimises the doctrine of Scripture.[2] Article 20 says we should not do this!

So does biblical theology have a high view of the Word of God *and* the Spirit of God?

WORD AND SPIRIT IN CREATION

Genesis 1 presents a description of creation involving both Word and Spirit. 'The Spirit of God was hovering over the waters' (v. 2) and, if there is any doubt whether the Hebrew word *ruach* (meaning 'breath', 'wind' or 'spirit') clearly implies the activity of God's Spirit in creation, there is added evidence that later Israelite writers thought it did.[3] For even if *ruach* was translated as 'wind of God' or 'breath of God' in these verses too, they seem to be a figurative way of referring to the action of God's Spirit in creation. This leads Wayne Grudem to conclude, 'The Holy Spirit was also at work in creation. He is generally pictured as completing, filling, and giving life to all creation.'[4] The brooding presence of the Spirit over the primeval creation is the prelude to all that follows.

The universe was created not only by the Spirit's initiation and supervision but at the word of God's command: 'And God said, "Let there be light," and there was light.'[5] God spoke, and it happened. This creative word is powerful and accomplishes that for which it was intended.[6] We know from the New Testament that this spoken Word of God in creation is identified with Jesus, the Word made flesh,[7] but in Genesis we are simply presented with the glorious truth that creation came into being as a double act of God's Word and God's Spirit. The precedent of partnership has been set.

WORD AND SPIRIT IN THE HISTORY OF ISRAEL

Following the disobedience of Adam and Eve and the consequent judgment on the whole human race, God sets in motion a grand rescue plan to save his broken world. It starts with the call of Abraham to be the father of a great nation: God enters into a solemn and everlasting covenant with him, through which all the nations will be blessed.[8] The rest of the Bible is the outworking of this gracious promise.

This is God's big metanarrative: the story of the patriarchs and their entry into Egypt, the call of Moses to lead the Israelites out of Egypt and through the wilderness into the promised land, the raising up of judges and kings, the provision of the tabernacle and the temple for worship and sacrifice, the conquests of Israel and Judah by foreign armies and their periods in exile and subsequent restoration. This is all treated by the biblical authors as 'sacred history', the story of God's unfolding purposes of salvation not only for Israel but for the whole world. There are very helpful overviews of this story in Vaughan Roberts' *God's Big Picture*,[9] Graeme Goldsworthy's *Gospel and Kingdom*,[10] and John Stott's *Understanding the Bible*.[11]

For our purposes, I want to highlight the two key agents of God in fulfilling his salvation purposes in the Old Testament: his Word and his Spirit. We have already seen that the universe came into existence by the word of God's command. We have now seen that the nation of Israel came into being by the word (or promise) of the covenant with Abraham. This nation was formed and shaped by the laws and commands given to Moses, especially the Ten Commandments, to govern their spiritual, moral and social life.[12] The Pentateuch (the first five books of the Bible) became the foundation of Israelite faith and hope, the historical books were the sacred record of Israel's chequered history, the wisdom literature became their guidance for godly living, the psalms were their hymn book for temple worship, and the prophets were the mouthpiece of God's searching critique and future hope. God ruled and governed his people through the growing corpus of Hebrew Scriptures. They revealed God's character and purposes, and they contained God's promises, God's wisdom, God's rebuke, God's hope and God's grace.[13] They kept the Israelites on track and brought them back when they wandered away. Times of spiritual revival were also times of rediscovering God's laws and recommitting themselves in joyful obedience.[14]

Yet that is not the whole story. It would also be true to say that God brought about his purposes in Israel's history through his Spirit. Griffith Thomas, in his book *The Holy Spirit of God*, describes the Holy Spirit as 'the executive of the Godhead',[15] the one who is supervising the unfolding plan of redemption. Professor Gordon Fee, in his masterly *God's Empowering Presence*,[16] identifies six ways in which the Holy Spirit's activity can be recognised in the Old Testament: as divine power, endowing humans with extraordinary powers;[17] as anointing leadership, equipping prophets, priests and kings with authority, power and wisdom;[18] as inspiring prophetic words through the prophets and other anointed leaders;[19] and, closely connected with prophetic inspiration, as the revelation of God's wisdom and purposes;[20] as the manifestation of God's presence;[21] and as the key to Israel's eschatological future, resting on the Messiah,[22] bringing salvation, renewal and blessing.[23]

We see in the Old Testament how the Word of God and the Spirit of God work together as God's agents in bringing about his redemptive purposes in and through the history of Israel.[24] It is the prelude for the further revelation of this salvation partnership, which is so clearly on display in the pages of the New Testament.

WORD AND SPIRIT IN THE MINISTRY OF JESUS

It is not an exaggeration to say that Jesus Christ is the focal point of the biblical metanarrative.[25] In him the covenantal promises to Abraham are fulfilled and the messianic hopes are met; he is the hope of Israel and the Saviour of the world.[26] He is the Lord from heaven who becomes the suffering servant, ministering to the poor and sick and outcasts, teaching and discipling his followers, and giving his life as a ransom and substitute for sinful people.[27] He rises again victoriously from the tomb as the first-fruit of God's new creation, conquering sin and death, commissioning the disciples for the task of world mission and then ascending back to heaven to rule at God's right hand.[28] God's eschatological future has begun now and awaits a final consummation when the Lord returns to establish justice and usher in a new heaven and earth. The kingdom of God is inaugurated and partially realised now, but the best is still to come.[29] In Christ the sin of Adam is undone, the effects of the fall are reversed and God is reclaiming his world. The gospel is the good news about Jesus Christ.[30]

There is a very clear partnership of Word and Spirit in the ministry of Jesus. His whole life and ministry were shaped by his study of the Hebrew Scriptures (the Old Testament), from which he came to understand his messianic role, and he submitted to the authority of the Scriptures not only in his life's mission but also in his theological debates with the Pharisees and Sadducees and in his personal conduct and ethical standards. He accepted unequivocally the divine inspiration of the Old Testament and he believed that it had an abiding and eternal authority.[31] In addition, he made provision for the writing of the New Testament in two ways: firstly, by promising that the coming Holy Spirit would 'teach you all things and... remind you of everything I have said to you';[32] and secondly, by appointing apostles with special authority and divine inspiration to provide an accurate record of Jesus' life and the Church's earliest beginnings (the Gospels and Acts) and to give a true interpretation of those events (the Epistles and Revelation). In short, Jesus endorsed the Scriptures in their entirety, both Old and New Testaments, as the inspired and authoritative Word of God, the definitive record and interpretation of God's plan of salvation.[33]

However, Jesus' life and ministry are shaped and directed not only by the Scriptures; the Spirit is also active at every stage. The Spirit who inspired the prophets to foretell the coming of the Messiah now ensures that all is fulfilled according to God's perfect planning.[34] He prepares the way by the miraculous birth of John the Baptist, who is filled with the Holy Spirit from his mother's womb, and will speak with the power and authority of a second Elijah to prepare Israel for the arrival of her Messiah.[35] He overshadows a young virgin in Palestine and causes her to conceive the divine Son of God; he prompts the prophecies of Simeon and Anna as they recognise Jesus' divine messiahship.[36] At Jesus' baptism, the Spirit descends on him like a dove following the Father's affirmation, and remains on him as his public ministry begins, and Luke (and Jesus) want us to see this as the messianic anointing of Isaiah 61:1–2.[37] Jesus' trials and temptations by Satan in the wilderness are prompted and orchestrated by the Spirit and Jesus returns to Nazareth 'in the power of the Spirit'.[38]

The Spirit-filled ministry that follows is presented by all three Synoptic Gospels as a manifestation of the kingdom of God in three ways: through proclamation and teaching in which God's truth shines forth and people are released from the darkness of ignorance and unbelief; through exorcism and deliverance in which God's rule is demonstrated and evil is banished; and through physical and spiritual healing in which God's wholeness (*shalom*) is experienced and the wounds of the fall are undone.[39] All of this flows out of the anointing of the Spirit on the Messiah, promised in Isaiah 61:1–2 and 11:1–5.

Then there is his greatest work still to happen, 'the hour' for which he came.[40] The same Spirit who led him into the wilderness now leads him into Gethsemane—and on to Calvary: 'Christ, who through the eternal Spirit, offered himself unblemished to God'.[41] Paul will later tell us that the Spirit was involved in the resurrection, too, raising him bodily from the grave and vindicating him as Son of God in defiance of the verdict of the Jewish court.[42] His ascension is the occasion for re-emphasising the coming gift of the Spirit upon his followers for the task of world mission.[43]

Throughout the life of Jesus, the Word and the Spirit were working in perfect harmony, anointing, orchestrating and enabling his messianic ministry at every stage. What God had joined together, Jesus was not going to divide.

WORD AND SPIRIT IN THE EARLY CHURCH

In the book of Acts, we are privileged to have not only a historical narrative of the spread of Christianity from its earliest beginnings but also a window into the life of the earliest Christian communities. Luke is keen to show that what started in Jerusalem with the death, resurrection and ascension of Jesus is now going to continue through his followers: 'In my former book, Theophilus, I wrote about all that Jesus began to do and to teach.'[44] Salvation had been won by Christ's saving work; it now needed to be shared with people around the globe, and this is the primary task of the Church.

In fulfilling this commission, the early Church was given two great resources: God's Word and God's Spirit. God's Word at this stage (before the writing of the New Testament and the closing of the canon of Scripture) was the Old Testament, the oral traditions of Jesus' teaching and the apostolic testimony to Jesus. The preaching and teaching of the apostles was the Spirit-inspired and authoritative interpretation of Jesus' ministry, often drawing heavily on the Old Testament, and there are many examples of these expositions.[45] Luke refers to this exposition of Christian truth in a variety of ways: as 'the apostles' teaching', 'the word of God', 'the good news of the kingdom of God' and 'the gospel'.[46] In fact, the 'Acts of the Apostles' could also be called the 'Progress of the Word of God' because when Luke wants to tell us that the church was growing, he tells us that 'the word of God spread', or 'all who lived in the province of Asia heard the word of the Lord'.[47] The Christians scattered by the persecution following Stephen's martyrdom 'preached the word wherever they went', and in Corinth Paul 'devoted himself exclusively to preaching, testifying to the Jews that Jesus was the Christ'.[48] When the apostles were in danger of getting distracted from this preaching and teaching ministry by an internal pastoral issue, they appointed seven deacons to distribute the provisions so that they could give their attention 'to prayer and the ministry of the word'.[49] When many in Samaria had become Christians, Luke tells us that they 'had accepted the word of God'.[50]

Woven into this ministry of the Word was the ministry of the Spirit. It is widely acknowledged by New Testament scholars that Luke's Gospel had a particular interest in the Holy Spirit, and this is hardly surprising if Luke was also the divinely appointed author of Acts, for the work of the Spirit is seen on every page. 'The Acts of the Holy Spirit' might also have been an appropriate title.[51] For example, the Spirit's coming in power is promised in Acts 1:8. In Acts 2:4 we read how he comes in power on the day of Pentecost, in fulfilment of the messianic promise in Joel 2:28–32, filling each of the disciples and enabling them to speak in other tongues. He is received by 3000 new believers after Peter's sermon in Acts 2:38–41. He refills the disciples after the prayer meeting in Acts 4:31, enabling them to speak the word of God with boldness. He is lied to by Ananias and Sapphira, and is the one who witnesses to the saving truth about Jesus, alongside the apostles. He is said to have filled the seven deacons and he fills Stephen (again) in preparation for his martyrdom.[52] He is received by the Samaritan converts when Peter and John place their hands on them.[53] He prompts Philip to approach the chariot of the Ethiopian, in order to lead him to Christ, and then takes Philip on to Azotus.[54] After Saul's conversion, Ananias prays for Paul to be 'filled with the Holy Spirit', and the church throughout Judea, Galilee and Samaria is 'strengthened and encouraged by the Holy Spirit'.[55] The Spirit directs Peter to go to the home of Cornelius, where he is able to lead the first Gentiles to Christ. The Holy Spirit comes on them in the same way that he came on the first disciples in Jerusalem, and Peter reminds them that this is the baptism of the Holy Spirit that John the Baptist had foretold.[56] The Spirit prompts Agabus to prophesy about a severe famine in Jerusalem, and the Spirit speaks directly to the church leaders at Antioch to release Paul and Barnabas for what will be Paul's first missionary journey.[57] The Holy Spirit is clearly 'director of operations', the executive of the Godhead, God on the move in all his sovereign power, spearheading the Church's mission.

It might be helpful, at this stage, to notice how Word and Spirit interact in three separate chapters in Acts, because this will help us to discern what Luke is trying to teach us. Acts 2 begins with an outpouring of God's Spirit upon the disciples, with accompanying spiritual gifts that glorify God and raise questions for the crowd (vv. 1–13). This calls for an explanation and results in a sermon: Peter's divinely inspired exposition of the life and ministry of Jesus (vv. 14–36). So the Spirit has led us to the Word. The Spirit is also speaking through the Word because the crowd are cut to the heart under a conviction of sin, and we know that this is the Spirit's work (v. 37).[58] The Spirit now uses Peter to instruct them in what they must do (v. 38), thus leading them back to the Word. But the

Word is now going to point them back to the Spirit, who can be received as the gift of God for all those who repent and believe in Christ (vv. 38–39). When they have received this gift of the Spirit, the Word then comes back into focus as they devote themselves to the apostles' teaching (v. 42). This teaching opens the way for community, worship, miracles, sacrificial giving and evangelism, all prompted and inspired by the Spirit (vv. 42–47). Commenting on this chapter, John Stott writes, 'It was through the apostolic preaching of God's Word in the power of the Spirit on the Day of Pentecost that the people of God became the Spirit-filled Body of Christ.'[59]

Let's take a closer look at Acts 13. As director of operations, the Holy Spirit speaks to the church leaders at Antioch, most probably through a prophetic message, telling them to set aside Paul and Barnabas for the work that God has prepared for them (vv. 1–2). The elders lay hands on them and pray, and they are sent on their way by the same Spirit (vv. 3–4). Arriving at Cyprus, 'they proclaimed the word of God in the Jewish synagogues' (v. 5). So the Spirit-prompted mission has now led into a ministry of the Word. The Spirit is powerfully at work in the ministry of the Word, eliciting opposition from Elymas the sorcerer, who is struck blind by a Spirit-filled command from Paul, for his opposition to the gospel (vv. 6–11). The Roman proconsul is watching all this and is 'amazed at the teaching about the Lord' (v. 12). Moving on to Perga in Pamphylia, the Spirit leads Paul and Barnabas into the synagogue for more teaching, and inspires Paul with an outstanding exposition of the Old Testament scriptures, pointing to Christ as the fulfilment of the Jewish hope (vv. 13–41). Many Jews believe, and the Christian missionaries are invited back the following Sabbath, with 'almost the whole city gathered to hear the word of the Lord' (vv. 42–44). Devout Jews become jealous of the impact of the gospel, so Paul turns his attention to the Gentiles, who 'were glad and honoured the word of the Lord' by believing (v. 48). Luke then gives us a Word and Spirit overview of what is going on: 'The word of the Lord spread through the whole region… And the disciples were filled with joy and the Holy Spirit' (see vv. 49–52).

Finally we will examine the interplay of Word and Spirit in Acts 20:17–38, as this passage has a particular relevance to church leaders. Paul arrives at Miletus and calls the Ephesian elders to meet him so that he can encourage them in their ministry before he leaves the district. He reminds them of the example of his own ministry, and his faithful preaching and teaching among them (vv. 20–21). His ministry is under the direction of the Holy Spirit, who compels him to go to Jerusalem but warns him of intense suffering (vv. 22–24). The focus has shifted from Word to Spirit, but now moves back to the ministry of the Word (vv. 25–27). But the Spirit is the one who has entrusted them with this pastoral ministry of caring for God's flock (v. 28); this ministry will involve protecting the flock from the 'savage wolves' (false teachers, see vv. 29–31), and so Paul points them back to 'the word of his grace' (v. 32) as their resource for ministry. The gathering ends with emotional scenes and prayer (vv. 36–38).

The book of Acts highlights how Word and Spirit work together in the early Church. The Spirit is the instigator, the one who illuminates the Scriptures and speaks powerfully through the preaching of the gospel, the glorifier of Christ, the giver of spiritual gifts, the worker of miracles and signs, the architect of Christian community. The Word is the divinely inspired teaching of the apostles, their exposition of the Hebrew Scriptures, their telling and interpreting of the saving work of Christ, and their application and instruction into the lives of those who believe. Word and Spirit work together inseparably for the cause of Christ, the growth of the kingdom and the building of the Church.

WORD AND SPIRIT IN THE NEW TESTAMENT EPISTLES

Does the rest of the New Testament support this view of the vital partnership? We will look briefly at the epistles of Paul, as space prevents a more extensive study.

Paul's epistles celebrate the gospel, the good news of Jesus Christ, and recognise the power of the gospel to bring people to faith in Christ.[60] He not only sees the Hebrew Scriptures as the divinely inspired Word of God but he also sees his own teaching (and that of his fellow apostles) as the Word of God.[61] It is 'the word of promise, 'the word of truth', 'the word of life', and 'the word of Christ'.[62] In his pastoral epistles especially, Paul urges young leaders (Timothy and Titus) to be ministers of the Word as their first and greatest priority, and to give themselves wholeheartedly to preaching and teaching the Word of God to their congregations.[63] For Paul knows the power of the Word to bring people to faith, to build up and sanctify God's people, and to equip them for ministry and service.[64]

But Paul is a theologian of the Spirit as well as the Word. You can't read his epistles and miss his emphasis on the Holy Spirit in the life of the believer, the corporate ministry of the local church and the task of Christian leadership. He saw the Holy Spirit as integral to the work of salvation, the guarantee and down-payment of our future inheritance.[65] You can't be a Christian without receiving the gift of the Spirit, and this initiation into Christ is the baptism of the Holy Spirit.[66] Our bodies are now a temple of the Holy Spirit and our conduct (particularly in the area of sexuality) must respect this sanctuary.[67] In fact, our whole lives should progressively display a growing holiness through the Spirit's indwelling presence— expressed as 'the fruit of the Spirit' and 'being transformed into his likeness with ever-increasing glory'.[68] The command to 'be filled with the Spirit'[69] is written in the context of needing wisdom and discipline for holy living. The Holy Spirit also has a corporate function, building the body of Christ through the gifts of the Spirit, strengthening the church with power for ministry and service, and inspiring the church's worship.[70] Finally, in addition to his instructions to the Ephesian elders,[71] Paul has more to say about the Holy Spirit to emerging church leaders in the Pastoral Epistles: there are no less than nine clear references to the Spirit's ministry in three short letters.[72]

What is Paul's wisdom for Timothy and Titus about the Holy Spirit and the work of Christian ministry? First, Paul says that Christian ministry originates in the call and gifting of the Holy Spirit[73] and, while there is a genuine debate over whether this refers to the initial gift of the Spirit or to some special gifting for ministry (such as the spiritual gift of teaching or leadership as in Romans 12:7–8), there is no doubt that Timothy is to 'stir it up' and 'fan it into flame'.[74] Second, Paul reminds Titus that the central blessing of the gospel, which he is called to preach, is the outpouring of the Holy Spirit.[75] This should not surprise us, because Peter said the same thing on the day of Pentecost, citing the prophet Joel.[76] But Paul may also be alluding to the new covenant passage in Ezekiel 36:25–27, where God promises to 'wash' his people with 'pure water' (cleansing from idolatry and all sinfulness) and then promises the gift of a new spirit, God's own Spirit. As Gordon Fee writes, 'The emphasis in Paul's sentence distinctly rests on the Spirit who is "lavishly poured out on us"... the Spirit not only renews, but in Pauline theology effects the washing away of sins and the making new of the believer's life'.[77] This is all 'through Jesus Christ our Saviour',[78] who won our salvation on the cross, but the task of applying it into the life of the believer is the work of the Spirit. Third, Paul reminds Timothy of the divine inspiration (and consequent authority) of the Scriptures, which he is called to preach and teach as his primary task. Gordon Fee again: 'Paul... shares with his Jewish heritage the conviction that the sacred scriptures were given by divine in-*spiration*, that is, by *the breath of God*, the Holy Spirit'.[79] He can therefore preach it with confidence in its power to change the lives of his hearers.

CONSEQUENCES

Biblical theology refuses to allow us to drive a wedge between the ministry of God's Spirit and the ministry of God's Word. As we have seen, the whole of Scripture bears eloquent testimony to the divinely forged partnership. Both are vital for Christian leaders and both must be embraced for the awesome task of Christian ministry.

Three theological consequences emerge from this biblical survey, around which all Christian believers, and most especially evangelicals, should agree: the sufficiency of the Scriptures, the sovereignty of the Spirit, and the supremacy of the Saviour.

The sufficiency of the Scriptures

We have seen how the Word of God is not only the unique revelation of God's being and character, but also the divinely inspired vehicle for bringing about God's saving purposes for his world. Under the Spirit's inspiration, the biblical authors have given us an entirely trustworthy and authoritative record of God's saving work through Christ. God has spoken through his Word, and God still speaks today as it is faithfully opened up and explained by preachers. To use Dr Jim Packer's immortal phrase, 'the Bible is God preaching'.[80]

All evangelicals, and especially those at the Charismatic end of the spectrum, need to be convinced of what the Reformers called 'the sufficiency of Scripture'. This does not mean that God never speaks outside of the medium of Scripture,[81] but it does mean that the reading and study of God's Word is the normative and most important way of hearing God's voice. Wayne Grudem, in his excellent chapter on the sufficiency of Scripture, defines it thus: 'The sufficiency of Scripture means that Scripture contained all the words of God he intended his people to have at each stage of redemptive history, and that it now contains everything we need God to tell us for salvation, for trusting him perfectly, and for obeying him perfectly'.[82] Rodman Williams, in his *Renewal Theology: Systematic Theology from a Charismatic Perspective*, is in complete agreement:

Special revelation was given through the Old Testament prophets, Jesus Christ and the early apostles. This revelation, centred in the Word made flesh, was prepared by the early prophets and completed by the early apostles. There is nothing more to be added: *God's truth has been fully declared. Accordingly, what occurs in revelation within the Christian community is* **not** *new truth that goes beyond the special revelation (if so it is spurious and not of God). It is only a deeper appreciation of what has already been revealed, or a disclosure of some message for the contemporary situation that adds nothing essentially to what He has before made known.*[83]

And again: 'In terms of that which is authoritative and therefore normative, what is written in Scripture always has the primacy. It tests and judges every affirmation of faith and doctrine'.[84]

After a large gathering of evangelicals at Blackpool for the fourth National Evangelical Anglican Congress (September 2003), John Coles (the leader of New Wine) wrote to all church leaders in the New Wine networks and said, 'I want to reiterate New Wine's belief in the authority of the Scriptures as expressed by Paul in writing to Timothy (2 Tim. 3:16–17)... our reference point in everything is the written word of God. It is against the written Word that all our ideas, talks, sermons and prophecies need to be weighed as to their truth.' He then challenged the New Wine leaders to preach the Word: 'The way some Charismatics preach, often anecdotally and thematically, rather than systematically and expositorally, has perhaps obscured the fact that the Scriptures are in all things the source of revelation and the touchstone of our reasoning'.[85]

The Bible is God's gift to his Church as the supreme source of authority and revelation for the Church today, and the all-sufficient resource for Christian ministry. Accordingly, Christian leaders must give themselves to preaching and teaching it as their primary responsibility.

The sovereignty of the Spirit

Our biblical survey has shown that the Spirit of God, from creation onwards, is sovereign over the world that God has made and the people whom God has called. He is 'the Lord, the giver of life who, with the Father and Son, is worshipped and glorified'.[86] He is the director of operations, the Comforter and Counsellor, the breath of God, the fire from heaven, the oil of anointing, the dove of peace, the glorifier of Jesus, the giver of spiritual gifts, and God's empowering presence. He is also the divine author of Scripture and the divine interpreter, who brings the Word of God into the hearts and lives of God's people.

How could we possibly do Christian ministry without him? How could we preach without his anointing and illumination? How could we lead a church without his wisdom and strength? How could we mobilise a congregation into mission without his empowering presence? How could we build up the body of Christ without his spiritual gifts? How could we grow into Christ's likeness without his fruit? How could we grow in our love for God unless he pours God's love into our hearts? We need him so much!

John Stott makes this point very forcibly in relation to our role of teaching and preaching the Bible. In *Calling Christian Leaders* (Chapter 3) he explores the relationship between Holy Spirit and Holy Scripture. Basing his exegesis on 1 Corinthians 2:6–16, he identifies four key roles of the Holy Spirit in relation to the Bible:

Firstly, he searches the depths of God and knows the thoughts of God, and is therefore uniquely qualified for his teaching role. Secondly, he revealed his findings to the apostles and the other biblical authors. Thirdly, he communicated those things through the biblical authors to others and did so in words chosen by him. Fourthly, he enlightens the minds of Bible readers to discern what he has revealed to and through the biblical authors, and continues this work of illumination today.[87]

He concludes: 'So we need to humble ourselves before both the Word and the Spirit. We still have to study the Word to ponder its meaning and application, but we also need to cry to the Holy Spirit for enlightenment... for the Word remains a dead letter until the Spirit brings it to life.'[88]

The supremacy of the Saviour

Finally, we should never forget that both Word and Spirit have a purpose beyond themselves. They both point to Christ. We have seen that the Old Testament points forward to Christ, eagerly anticipating his coming, and the New Testament points back to Christ, giving us the definitive explanation of who he was, why he came and how we can know him. We have also seen how the Spirit spoke through the Law and the Prophets, bearing witness to a coming king, and how he inspired the apostles in their testimony to Jesus, leading them into all truth, enshrining that truth in the pages of the New Testament and revealing that truth to us today as the Bible is taught. Neither Word nor Spirit is there for itself; each has the higher purpose of exalting Christ.

If the Word of God and the Spirit of God are God's way of pointing to Christ as the unique Saviour of the world, then that is the best possible reason for embracing both in our calling as Christian leaders. But, we might ask, is there a precedent for this? Are there other Christian leaders down the centuries who have done it, and what has been the impact of their ministries? That is the subject of the next chapter.

Notes

1   In his article 'Moore Theology: A Friendly Critique', Philip Eveson highlights the views of John Woodhouse, the Principal of Moore College, Sydney, who

argues that the Spirit is so wedded to the Word that, whenever the Bible is preached, the Spirit is invariably at work. He comments, 'The Moore view is that there is no need to pray for unction, for some special anointing of the Spirit on preacher or people. The Spirit is automatically at work when the Word of God is opened... Woodhouse has gone too far and so identified Word and Spirit that the Spirit has no separate identity and function. This has been a Moore characteristic and must be seen as a serious departure from the Puritan and Evangelical teaching of the past. Because of their fear of Charismatic influences they have reinterpreted texts of Scripture to silence any suggestion of a direct work of the Spirit' (*Foundations*, Autumn 2006, p. 28).

2   Although J. Rodman Williams' *Renewal Theology* (Zondervan, 1996) is a magisterial work of biblical theology, it is a pity that it lacks a separate chapter on the doctrine of Scripture as the Word of God; instead it is found in a sub-section under 'Special revelation' (Vol. 1, pp. 36–43). Contrast Wayne Grudem's *Systematic Theology* (IVP, 1994), whose opening section is 'Part 1: The Doctrine of the Word of God'. Likewise, Williams' high view of preaching and teaching the Word is found in a subsection of 'Ministry' (Vol. 3, pp. 181–186) and so loses some of its impact.

3   Job 33:4; Psalm 104:30; Job 26:13; Isaiah 40:13

4   Grudem, *Systematic Theology*, p. 267

5   Genesis 1:3

6   Psalm 33:6, 9

7   John 1:1–3, 14; Colossians 1:16

8   Genesis 12:1–3

9   Vaughan Roberts, *God's Big Picture* (IVP, 2003)

10   Graeme Goldsworthy, *Gospel and Kingdom* (Paternoster, 1981)

11   John Stott, *Understanding the Bible* (SU, revised 1984) (ch. 3)

12   Exodus 20:1–21; Joshua 1:8; Psalm 119 and so on

13   Psalm 19

14   2 Chronicles 34:14–33

15   W.H. Griffith Thomas, *The Holy Spirit of God* (Church Room Press, 1974), p. 16

16   Gordon Fee, *God's Empowering Presence* (Hendrickson, 1994), pp. 905–910

17   Exodus 31:3–4; Judges 14:6; Daniel 5:14; 1 Samuel 10:10

18   Numbers 11:17; 27:18; Judges 3:10; 6:34; 11:29; 1 Samuel 11:6; 16:13

19   Numbers 11:25–26, 29; 2 Samuel 23:2; 1 Chronicles 12:18; 2 Chronicles 15:1; 20:14; Joel 2:28–29; Micah 3:8; Zechariah 7:12

20   Isaiah 11:2; Daniel 4:8–9, 18; 5:11, 14

21   Psalm 139:7; Isaiah 63:10–14; Ezekiel 36:27; 37:14; Haggai 2:5; Zechariah 4:6

22   Isaiah 11:2; 42:1; 59:21; 61:1

23   Ezekiel 11:19; 18:31; 36:26–27; 37:1–14; Joel 2:28–30

24   This conclusion is reinforced by Dr James Robson, Senior Tutor in Old
     Testament at Wycliffe Hall, in the published version of his doctoral thesis, *Word
     and Spirit in Ezekiel* (Library of Hebrew Bible/ Old Testament Studies, T&T Clark,
     2006). He writes, 'In the Old Testament, two fundamental experiences of God
     are these: an encounter with the "word" of God… and an encounter with the
     "spirit" or "wind" or "breath" of God… Encounters with Yahweh's word and
     Yahweh's spirit are central to the prophet Ezekiel and to the book that bears his
     name' (p. 3).

25   Luke 24:25–27

26   Galatians 3:29; Romans 4:16; Acts 2:36; John 3:16

27   Philippians 2:6–11; Mark 10:45; John 13:1–13

28   1 Corinthians 15:1–58; Acts 1:1–11

29   Revelation 21:1–5; 1 Peter 1:3–5

30   Romans 5:15–17; Romans 1:1–3

31   Luke 10:26; Mark 12:10; Mark 7:9, 13; Mark 12:24, 36; Matthew 4:4;
     Matthew 5:17–18

32   John 14:25–26

33   1 Corinthians 1:1; 1 Peter 1:1; 1 John 1:1; Hebrews 1:1–3; 2:3–4

34   Galatians 4:4

35   Luke 1:15; Malachi 3:1; Luke 2:17

36   Luke 1:35; 2:25–32, 36–38

37   Luke 3:21–22; John 1:29–32; Luke 4:17–21

38   Luke 4:1, 14

39   Mark 1:13–14, 21–28, 29–34

40   John 17:1

41   Hebrews 9:14

42   1 Timothy 3:16; Romans 1:4

43   Acts 1:8

44   Acts 1:1

45   See, for example, Acts 2:14–36; 3:11–26; 4:8–12; 7:1–53

46   Acts 2:42; 4:31; 8:12, 25

47   Acts 6:7; 19:10

48   Acts 8:4; 18:5

49   Acts 6:2–4

50   Acts 8:14

51   The clearest recent statement of this partnership between Word and Spirit in
     Acts is in Colin Martyn and Tony Payne, *The Trellis and the Vine* (Matthias Media,
     2009): 'We call it the Acts of the Apostles, but a better name would perhaps
     be "The Acts of the Word and the Spirit of God through the Apostles", because

that's how it seems to go. The apostolic task is to preach; to bear witness; to proclaim the word; and to do so under the power and enabling of God's Spirit' (p. 36).

52 Acts 6:3; 7:54
53 Acts 8:17
54 Acts 8:29–40
55 Acts 9:17, 31
56 Acts 10:19; 11:15–16
57 Acts 11:27–28; 13:2
58 Compare John 16:8
59 John Stott, *I Believe in Preaching* (Hodder and Stoughton, 1982), p. 110
60 Romans 1:1–4, 16
61 2 Timothy 3:16; 1 Thessalonians 2:13; 1 Corinthians 7:10; 1 Thessalonians 5:12–13; 2 Timothy 4:1
62 Romans 9:9 (NKJV); Ephesians 1:13; 2 Corinthians 6:7 (NKJV); Philippians 2:16; Colossians 3:16
63 1 Timothy 4:11–13; 2 Timothy 4:1–2; Titus 2:1–10
64 2 Timothy 3:15–17; see also Acts 20:32
65 Ephesians 1:13–14; 2 Corinthians 5:5
66 Ephesians 1:13–14; 2 Corinthians 5:5; Romans 5:5; 8:9; 1 Corinthians 12:13
67 1 Corinthians 6:18–19
68 Galatians 5:22; 2 Corinthians 3:17–18
69 Ephesians 5:18
70 Romans 12:3–8; 1 Corinthians 12:1–13; Ephesians 4:7–16; 3:14–20; 5:18–19
71 Acts 20:13–38
72 For a careful consideration of each of these, see Fee, *God's Empowering Presence*, pp. 755–795.
73 1 Timothy 1:18; 4:14; 2 Timothy 1:6
74 2 Timothy 1:6
75 Titus 3:5–8
76 Acts 2:14–21
77 Fee, *God's Empowering Presence*, p. 782
78 Titus 3:6
79 Fee, *God's Empowering Presence*, p. 793
80 Quoted in Stott, *I Believe in Preaching*, p. 103
81 Scripture itself tells us to listen for God's voice in creation (Psalm 19:1–4; Romans 1:19–20), through conscience (Psalm 51:3–6; 1 John 1:8–9), through godly advice from trusted friends and loved ones (Proverbs 6:20–21; 22:17), through circumstances (Philippians 1:12–14) and through spiritual gifts (Acts 11:27; 1 Corinthians 12:7–11; 14:24–25). But these should never be seen as

an alternative to Scripture, or contradicting or adding to it. In fact, they should take us to the Scriptures for testing, clarity and understanding. This area will be looked at in more detail in Chapter 7.

82 Grudem, *Systematic Theology*, p. 127

83 Rodman Williams, *Renewal Theology*, p. 44

84 Rodman Williams, *Renewal Theology*, p. 23

85 John Coles, *New Wine Networks Bulletin* (2003/13)

86 The Nicene Creed

87 John Stott, *Calling Christian Leaders* (IVP, 2002), p. 82

88 Stott, *Calling Christian Leaders*, p. 82

HISTORICAL PERSPECTIVES

In one sense, every Christian is a Word and Spirit person. We become a Christian by hearing the gospel as it is explained from the Scriptures and we receive the Spirit as the indwelling gift of God when we come to Christ. Most Christians continue to grow in their relationship with the Lord through the Word and the Spirit: the Bible is our spiritual food, which helps us to grow, and the Spirit is our power supply, strengthening us to live the Christian life. It would be very easy, therefore, to lay claim to the entire Christian heritage and boldly state that all of it bears eloquent witness to the partnership of Word and Spirit!

The historian in me, however, requires a greater degree of historical integrity. I want to resist the temptation to squeeze the whole of church history through the funnel of Word and Spirit; instead, I want to let certain parts of Christian history speak for themselves and then leave you to make up your own mind if there is a precedent for holding Word and Spirit together in Christian leadership. The criteria for selecting these historical snapshots are the ones I mentioned at the end of the last chapter, namely the sufficiency of the Scriptures (their full inspiration, their supreme authority and the priority of preaching), the sovereignty of the Spirit (his orchestration of church growth, his inspiration and illumination of the Scriptures, his empowering presence and his equipping of the body of Christ with spiritual gifts) and the supremacy of the Saviour (both Word and Spirit having a purpose beyond themselves, to glorify Christ and advance his kingdom).

THE CHURCH FATHERS

The 'Apostolic Fathers', as they were also known, were the promi-
nent church leaders who succeeded the New Testament apostles,
and they ministered between AD80 and 400 approximately (generally known as the patristic period, after *pater*, the Latin for 'father').
We find in them an important continuity with the biblical emphasis
on Word and Spirit.

In his historical sketch of the glory of preaching,[1] John Stott
finds in their writings and activities a strong emphasis on preaching
and teaching the Word of God. *The Didache*, for example, written
around the beginning of the second century AD as a church manual
on ethics and ministry, refers to a variety of teaching and preaching
ministries. If a teacher contradicts the apostolic faith or fails to
practise what he preaches, he is a false prophet (11:1–2; 12:1–5).
If he is genuine, he must be listened to with humility: 'My child,
him that speaketh to thee the Word of God remember him night
and day; and thou shalt honour him as the Lord' (4:1).[2] Similarly,
Justin Martyr's *First Apology* (written in the middle of the second
century) defends Christianity to the Emperor and describes the
weekly worship of the Christians, which highlights the centrality of
reading and teaching the Scriptures: 'And on the day called Sunday,
all who live in cities or in the country gather together to one place,
and the memoirs of the Apostles or the writings of the prophets are
read, as long as time permits; then when the reader has ceased, the
president verbally instructs, and exhorts to the imitation of these
good things.'[3]

The Latin father Tertullian, at the end of the second century, wrote
his *Apology* to clear Christians of false accusations, and described
again the importance of the Scriptures in Christian gatherings: 'We
assemble to read our sacred writings... With the sacred words we
nourish our faith, we animate our hope, we make our confidence
more steadfast... In the same place also exhortations are made.'[4]
One further example, from the late patristic period, is that of

49

John Chrysostom, who became the Bishop of Constantinople in AD398, after preaching for twelve years in the cathedral at Antioch. Preaching on Ephesians 6, he likened the body of Christ to a human body that is subject to disease and sickness. How can Christ's body be healed? 'One only means and one way of cure has been given to us... and that is the teaching of the Word... this serves instead of medicine... and without it nothing else will avail'.[5] A century after his death, his greatness as a preacher was formally recognised: 'He is generally and justly regarded as the greatest pulpit orator of the Greek Church. Nor has he any superior or equal among the Latin Fathers.'[6]

The person and work of the Holy Spirit features in the writings and convictions of the Church Fathers, certainly in terms of the Spirit's inspiration and illumination of Scripture, and also in the use of spiritual gifts. Barnabas and Clement both emphasise the Spirit as the inspirer of the Old Testament and the apostolic teaching.[7] Irenaeus, in countering the claims of the Montanists to 'special revelations' that had a supposed authority above the Scriptures, stated that 'all knowledge was revealed in Jesus and passed down apostolically to the Church. The Spirit never gave new truths, but bears witness to the Truth.'[8] Tertullian in the West and Origen in the East both contributed theologically to the creedal definitions of the Spirit in relation to the Trinity. There is also clear evidence during this period of the continuing use of the New Testament spiritual gifts.[9] For example, Justin Martyr, in his *Second Apology* (c.153), wrote about exorcism: 'For numberless demoniacs throughout the whole world, and in your city, many of our Christian men exorcising them in the name of Jesus Christ... have healed and do heal.'[10] Irenaeus also spoke of true exorcisms, prophecies and healings while refuting the heresies of Gnosticism:

For some do certainly and truly drive out devils, so that those who have been cleansed from evil spirits frequently join themselves to the Church. Others have foreknowledge of things to come: they see visions, and utter prophetic expressions. Others still heal the sick by laying hands upon them, and they are made whole... It is not possible to name the number of gifts which the Church, (scattered) throughout the whole world, has received from God, in the name of our Lord Jesus Christ.[11]

Similarly, Tertullian wrote in *To Scapula* (Chap. 5): 'How many men of rank (to say nothing of common people) have been delivered from devils, and healed of diseases!'[12] And Novatian of Rome (AD210–280), who gave the Western Church its first theological articulation of the Trinity, writes about the ongoing work of the Spirit in the third century AD, in Chapter 29 of his *Treatise Concerning the Trinity*:

This is he who places prophets in the Church, instructs teachers, directs tongues, gives powers and healings, does wonderful works, offers discrimination of spirits, affords powers of government, suggests counsels, and orders and arranges whatever other gifts there are of **charismata**; *and thus makes the Lord's Church, everywhere and in all, perfected and completed.*[13]

It seems to me that any plain, unbiased reading of the early Church Fathers shows that they witnessed, and indeed encouraged, an ongoing ministry of the Word and the Spirit in direct continuity with biblical theology in general and the New Testament church in particular.

THE MIDDLE AGES

During the Middle Ages (approximately AD400–1500) there were certainly faithful church leaders who tried to hold on to both Word and Spirit (as we shall see), as well as some important developments in theological and philosophical thinking. The Church continued to spread throughout the world, but at the same time it began to lose something of the vitality of New Testament Christianity. Jesus was still building his Church, but by the end of this period it was in need of reformation in order to bring it back to its roots.

A whole raft of factors have been identified by church historians as contributing to the gradual decline of spiritual life and vitality during this period: the establishment of Christianity as the official state religion of the Roman Empire; the compromising nature of partnerships with civil authorities in the bid for power, wealth and prestige; the corruption and worldliness of a significant proportion of the clergy; the acceptance of some non-biblical concepts, which served to undermine the central gospel truths; the use of Greek philosophical rationalism in Christian apologetics; the over-formalisation of the Church's liturgical practices and the increasing clericalisation of the church, which focused the task of ministry with increasing exclusivity upon the ordained professionals instead of upon the whole body of Christ.[14]

Even so, there remained some outstanding figures in the Christian history of this period. St Augustine of Hippo, widely recognised as the Father of Western Christianity and the greatest theologian among the Latin Fathers, was certainly a person of Word and Spirit. He had a high view of the Bible, influenced by Bishop Ambrose of Milan, under whose preaching and teaching he came to faith. Augustine stressed the unity of Old and New Testaments, arguing that they both bear witness to the same God of grace, even if they are written in different forms of expression: 'The New Testament is hidden in the Old; and the Old is made accessible by the New'.[15] McGrath observes that this text became of major importance in the subsequent history of biblical interpretation, particularly in connection with the relationship between the Old and New Testaments. Augustine also developed a way of interpreting the Bible that distinguished between the literal/historical sense and the allegorical/spiritual sense. So to understand the Old Testament at a purely historical level was not enough; a deeper spiritual interpretation was needed to grasp its full meaning. As a Bible scholar, Augustine devoted his service to God as Bishop of Hippo, writing numerous letters, treatises, books and sermons. His two most well-known books are his *Confessions*, a personal record of his spiritual journey and his experience of God's undeserved grace, and *The City of God*, in which he wrestled with the issues raised by the fall of Rome in AD410.

But Augustine was a man of the Spirit as well as the Word. It is less well known that his biggest work was a monumental 15 volumes on the Trinity, written over 20 years. Here he not only spelt out the equal divinity of each of the persons of the Trinity but also developed a theology of the Spirit as the 'Love Gift' of the Father and the Son. The love that is shared between the Father and the Son is mediated to the Christian through the ministry of the Holy Spirit (Romans 5:5) and Christians therefore should reciprocate by loving one another. Also, in Book 22, chapter 28 of *The City of God* he states his belief in the ongoing work of the Spirit in miracles and exorcism: 'It is sometimes objected that the miracles, which Christians claim to have occurred, no longer happen… the truth is that even today miracles are being wrought in the name of Christ.'[16] Then he makes a long list of some of those he knows about, including a blind man whose sight was restored, a woman in Carthage healed of breast cancer, a doctor healed of gout, a young girl in Hippo delivered of demons and the resuscitation of a nun.

Another positive Christian development in the Middle Ages was the growth of monasticism. From its earliest appearances in the third and fourth centuries, it arose as a reaction to the increasing worldliness of the Church, and out of the desire to live a godly, simple and disciplined life in the service and worship of God. Three figures stand out as especially anointed by God with a wholehearted devotion to Christ, and all three were people of the Word and the Spirit. Firstly, Benedict of Nursia (480–547) was the founder of the Benedictine Order and his *Rule of Benedict* became the key text of Western monasticism. The three main activities of the monasteries (resourced by the Word and the Spirit) were the regular and systematic reading of the Scriptures, the daily offering of praise and worship, and the disciplined habit of corporate and private prayer.

Secondly, Bernard of Clairvaux (1090–1153) was raised up by God in the twelfth century to form a new monastic order, which became known as the Cistercians. Bernard had been fired by a vision in which he saw a whole valley of men of every age streaming towards the monastery, and he learnt to trust in God's provision for the founding of this new order. He based it on the original Benedictine rule, and his White Monks (so called because of the colour of their habit) were to seek God in simplicity, silence and poverty. It was a prophetic challenge to the compromised faith of many churches and other monastic communities. Bernard was a powerfully attractive personality and was so successful at recruiting people for the monastic life that mothers were said to have hidden their sons when he was around. He was a fine and eloquent preacher, always bringing a message of God's infinite love for humanity and calling for people to love God intimately in return. He expressed these convictions in his writings, too, especially in his meditations on the Song of Songs, which he interpreted as an allegory of the intimate love between Christ and the Church.

Thirdly, Francis of Assisi (1182–1226), the founder of the Franciscan Order, was also a Word and Spirit person. He had been struck by the Gospel reading where Jesus sends out his disciples to go and preach the gospel, instructing them not to take any money or extra clothing (Matthew 10). Francis declared, 'This is what I long to do with all my heart.' So, wearing just a rough grey tunic with a cord round his waist, he went around preaching a simple message of God's love in Christ and calling people to repentance. Others quickly followed his inspiring example. Alongside the impact of his apostolic preaching ministry was a ministry of prayer for the sick, and a vast number of healings are associated with his travels. Here is an account of just one of them:

Once when the holy man of God, Francis, was going about through various regions to preach the Kingdom of God, he came to a certain city called Toscanella. There… a certain soldier of that city gave him hospitality; he had an only son who was lame and weak in body… The

54

father... cast himself at his feet, begging health for his son... [Francis]
prayed and then put his hand upon the boy and, blessing him, raised him
up. Immediately, with all present looking on and rejoicing, the boy arose
completely restored and began to walk here and there about the house.[17]

It seems that the Spirit was at work through his prayers as well as his preaching.

In addition to these three inspirational figures, there were also the missionary monks who were responsible, under God, for the conversion of the British Isles in the fifth and sixth centuries: St Patrick (390–461), the apostle to the Irish; St Columba (521–597), the Irish missionary to Scotland; and St David (c.500–589), the renowned preacher and teacher who founded monasteries and churches in Wales. Thus, Celtic Christianity played a key part in the forwarding of God's kingdom, and it is important to notice that woven into it were the twin cords of Word and Spirit.[18] Also, St Augustine of Canterbury (d. 604) and his small band of monks from Rome arrived in the south of England and baptised 'many thousands' of Anglo-Saxon converts, according to Pope Gregory in his letter to Bishop Eulogios. It is worth noting that Augustine's strategy was to 'imitate the apostolic life of the primitive Church, in continued prayers, fastings and vigils' and 'in preaching the word of life'. In time, even Ethelbert, the most powerful pagan king in the south of England, was converted to Christ and baptised, probably at Easter 601 in St Martin's Church, Canterbury. He had been impressed by the 'pure and holy life' of the missionaries, and had been convinced of the superiority of the Christian God after witnessing some miracles.

We also ought to mention three theologians and the impact of their philosophical theology at a time when rationalism and reason reigned supreme in the intellectual schools of Europe. Anselm of Canterbury (1033–1109) used logic and reason to argue the case for the existence of God and to set out a rational explanation of the atonement. Peter Abelard (1079–1142), similarly, was a powerful advocate of this new kind of philosophical theology, applying logic and dialectic to matters of faith and laying the foundations of a university style of education, with a number of courses laid on by a number of masters in one city. Thomas Aquinas (1225–74) also employed reason and logic in defending the Christian faith, writing commentaries and systematic theologies, developing arguments for the existence of God and producing a rationale for Christian ethics based on natural law. These scholastic theologians defended Christian truth using the intellectual thought-forms of their day and helped pave the way for the study of theology as an academic discipline in universities. The study of the Bible was the focal point of medieval theology, and the Spirit of God was continuing to uphold and defend the existence and reality of God.

One final figure needs attention: John Wycliffe (1329–84) has been hailed, quite justifiably, as the 'Morning Star of the Reformation'. He was a priest and lecturer at Oxford University, and he was first and foremost a man of the Word of God. His convictions about the authority of the Bible led him to teach that it should be the source of all Christian doctrine and that it could be read and understood without the need for the Church's interpretation, which was a radical concept at the time. He was also determined to produce a version of the Bible in vernacular English so that everyone could read it, and he began a translation from the Latin into a Midland dialect. The 'Wyclif Bible' became the first full English version and it paved the way for others. Wycliffe was also a prophetic figure, trying to listen to what the Spirit was saying to the contemporary church and fearlessly bringing a challenging critique. He denounced clerical abuses and believed that the church could forfeit its authority through sin. He dared to suggest that the Bible and the church might be at odds with each other over the doctrine of transubstantiation. His bold prophetic ministry not only inspired the Lollards and the Hussites but also paved the way for a deeper and more radical reform of the Church than he could ever have imagined.

THE REFORMATION PERIOD

The Church of the late Middle Ages was in desperate need of spiritual reform and renewal. Historians have identified a wide range of weaknesses in it, which led to the Protestant revolution that exploded when Martin Luther nailed his 95 Theses to the church door at Wittenberg in 1517.

The Reformation period (1500–1700) was fundamentally about a rediscovery of the Bible.[19] Through Luther's study of Romans and his rediscovery of the Pauline doctrine of justification by faith alone, due to God's amazing grace in Christ, he said: 'I felt myself absolutely born again. The gates of paradise had been flung open and I had entered. There and then the whole of Scripture took on a new look to me.' These scriptural discoveries caused him to challenge the Roman Church about obscuring the gospel message through some of its rituals and ceremonies. When called to recant on his criticisms and his challenge to papal authority at the Diet of Worms in April 1521, his reply was to become legendary: 'Unless I am convinced by Scripture or clear reason—for I do not trust the Pope or church councils—I am bound by the Scriptures I have quoted. My conscience is held captive by the Word of God.'[20]

As events unfolded and Luther parted company with Rome and began to form his own congregations of 'Protestants', the new churches shaped themselves round the preaching and exposition of the Scriptures, and now the administration of the sacraments was valid only after the Word of God had been taught. For 'the Church owes its life to the Word of promise, and is nourished and preserved by this same Word—the promises of God make the Church, not the Church the promises of God.'[21] It is therefore indispensible for our growth in the Christian life: 'The soul can do without all things except the Word of God... If it has the Word it is rich and lacks nothing, since this Word is the Word of life, of truth, of light, of peace, of righteousness, of salvation, of joy, of liberty.'[22] Why so? Because the Bible is all about Christ, so 'to preach Christ means to feed the soul, to make it righteous, to set it free and to save it, if it believe the preaching.'[23]

Luther was also a man of the Spirit in many ways. He believed that the Spirit of God indwells the believer and brings God's grace and forgiveness into our lives. He believed in the Spirit's work of giving assurance and promoting sanctification, and he believed that the Spirit brings God's grace to us through the sacraments when they are administered faithfully and received by faith. He also believed in the Spirit's inspiration of the Bible and his illuminating ministry in the preaching and teaching of God's Word. Also, although he believed that the gifts of the Spirit had ceased with the closing of the apostolic era and that miracles should no longer be expected as the Church was now established, he did encourage prayer for the sick, quoting Mark 16:17–18,[24] and he also believed that God had used him in this ministry, including a time when he prayed for his closest companion, Melanchthon, when he was very sick, and God graciously answered his prayers.[25]

Luther was extremely disturbed by the claims of the radical Anabaptists to 'spiritual revelations' outside and beyond the boundaries of scriptural revelation, and he vehemently opposed these 'heavenly prophets', as he sarcastically called them.[26] Yet he was not completely opposed to the ministry of the Spirit in inspiring godly thoughts in prayer from meditations on the Scriptures. For example, he gives instructions to a local barber on how to pray using the Lord's Prayer. Having explained how to interpret each of the petitions, Luther then encourages his friend to listen carefully to the voice of the Holy Spirit: 'If such an abundance of good thoughts come to us we ought to disregard the other petitions, make room for such thoughts, listen in silence, and under no circumstance obstruct them. The Holy Spirit himself preaches here, and one word of his sermon is far better than a thousand of our prayers.'[27]

The second phase of the Reformation was presided over by John Calvin (1509–64), who provided the Reformed faith with a systematic theological framework, particularly through his mammoth *Institutes of the Christian Religion*. For this reason he is called 'the Father of Reformed and Presbyterian doctrine and theology'.[28] His ideas were absorbed and developed by Reformed theologians across Europe, and his influence can be clearly seen in the creedal confessions of Christian faith and practice such as the Heidelberg Catechism (1563) and the Westminster Confession (1647). Like Luther, his motto was *Sola Scriptura* (Scripture Only) and, from his base in Geneva, he set about expounding biblical doctrine in a systematic way. Since the Bible is the ultimate source of authority for the Church, all church teaching, tradition and practice must come under its scrutiny. So, according to the Institutes, the first and major mark of a true church is the faithful preaching of the Word: 'Wherever we see the Word of God purely preached and heard... there, it is not to be doubted, a Church of God exists.'[29] It is a glorious statement of the centrality of the ministry of the Word, and the priority of preaching within the Evangelical movement today has been deeply shaped by this giant theologian of the Reformed faith.

Interestingly, Calvin has also been called 'the Theologian of the Holy Spirit', not because he majored on the person of the Holy Spirit to the exclusion of other aspects of Christian theology, and not because he differed in substance from Luther or the other leading continental Reformers on the whole subject. Like them, he placed the emphasis on the Spirit's work in relation to Scripture, Christ, grace, faith, salvation and holiness. There are several reasons why he has been given this title (quite justifiably). Firstly, he was the first Church theologian since the patristic period to produce a full and systematic theology of the Holy Spirit in relation to the whole of the Christian life, relating the experience and application of salvation to the working of the Holy Spirit. For Protestants, this inner testimony of the Holy Spirit replaced the Roman doctrine of the Church as the source of assurance and salvation. Secondly, Calvin set salvation firmly in a trinitarian context, insisting that salvation is the organic work of the triune Godhead, the Father choosing (election), the Son redeeming (redemption) and the Holy Spirit renewing (regeneration). Thirdly, while he accepted the

Western tradition of the Trinity as the unity of love, he injected 'long forgotten life into that theology by his emphasis on the old biblical idea of the Spirit as God in action'.[30] For him, the primary ministry of the Spirit was activating the redemptive purposes of the Father and the Son, and this ministry is exercised through the preaching of the Word of God, as the Spirit brings an internal enlightenment to the believer.[31] Like Luther, he opposed the supposed private 'revelations' of the radical Anabaptists, partly on the grounds of their disconnection of the Spirit's work from the Word of God and partly because he believed that the gifts of the Spirit were temporary (for the apostolic age only). However, he did not rule out the possibility of miracles still happening today, and even seems sure that he knows of them occurring: 'God's name ought always and everywhere be hallowed, whether by miracles or by the natural order of things... we are not entirely lacking in miracles, and those very certain and not subject to mockery.'[32] Also, there is clear evidence that spiritual gifts were used by his followers, most notably in the development of the Reformed faith in Scotland presided over by John Knox[33] and the Calvinist Huguenots in France, led by Antoine Marcourt and Henry of Navarre.[34] Paul Helm, who teaches philosophy and theology at Regent College, Vancouver, has concluded that Calvin's theology of the Church had a 'central motif of Word and Spirit'.[35]

The Puritans, standing in direct continuity with Luther and Calvin and the Reformed faith, were also people who valued the Word and the Spirit. As Mark Noll described them, 'From William Tyndale the Puritans took an intense commitment to Scripture and a theology which emphasised the concept of covenant; from John Knox they absorbed a dedication to thorough reform in church and state; and from John Hooper they received a determined conviction that Scripture should regulate ecclesiastical structure and personal behaviour alike'.[36] They emerged in the late 16th and early 17th centuries in England, Ireland and Scotland, and they basically split into two groupings: those who stayed within the established church and pursued further godly reformation from within, and those who decided (or were forced) to leave and form their own separatist denominations. Herein lay the roots of English non-conformity.

The Puritans, with their deep roots in Calvinism, were first and foremost preachers of the Bible. Irvonwy Morgan's research into *The Godly Preachers of the Reformation Settlement* (1965) concluded, 'The essential thing in understanding the Puritans was that they were preachers before they were anything else... What bound them together... was their consciousness that they were called to preach the Gospel... Puritan tradition in the first and last resort must be assessed in terms of the pulpit.'[37] A good example of this can be found in the spiritual classic *The Reformed Pastor* (1656) by the Puritan divine Richard Baxter. Here he briefs other pastors as to their primary responsibility: 'In a word, we much teach them, as much as we can, of the word and works of God... All Christians are disciples or scholars of Christ; the church is his school, we are his ushers; the Bible is his grammar; this is it that we must be daily teaching them'.[38] But in the Puritan love for the Bible we should not miss their love for the Holy Spirit, too, as Simon Ponsonby elaborates in his chapter on 'The Spirit and the Word'.[39] The Puritan divine John Owen, adviser to Cromwell and Vice-chancellor of Oxford University, wrote a major theological treatise on the Holy Spirit,[40] where he spelt out the Spirit's role in the life of the believer. In our response to the gospel, it is the Spirit who applies the saving work of Christ to us. As an illustration of this, he cites the example of the Ethiopian eunuch: he needed Philip to open the Scripture but he needed the Holy Spirit to open his heart. Similarly, the Puritan Richard Sibbes spoke of God's wonderful gift of 'Double Light': the Spirit in the Scripture *and* the Spirit in the believer. But the personal 'revelations' of the Spirit must be in complete harmony with the inspired Word, for 'the Spirit doth not breathe contrary notions... the Spirit goes along with the word and makes it work'.[41]

It seems, then, that the Puritans not only held to the centrality and primacy of the Bible but also had a good theology of the Spirit and an experience of 'the imminent hand of God', not least in spiritual apprehensions and special providences. The evidence for this is in their journals.[42] It is worth noting Simon Ponsonby's astute observation of the whole Reformation period: 'The radical reformers seriously erred by abandoning the Word for the Spirit... The reformers were rather too restricting, subordinating the Spirit to the Word... The Puritans found the middle way, truly holding Word and Spirit together.'[43]

Before we leave the Reformation period, it is humbling to recognise that God used this rediscovery of the gospel to bring about a measure of reform and renewal in the Roman Catholic Church itself. Although this is traditionally known as the 'Counter-Reformation', implying that these reforms were purely a reaction to the emergence of Protestantism (which they were, in part), scholars are increasingly referring to them as the 'Catholic Reformation', because they were aimed at addressing the widespread abuses of power and authority in the late medieval Catholic Church. Although the Council of Trent (1545–63) reaffirmed traditional Catholic teaching in almost all respects, there were some positive aspects: the trade in indulgences was reformed considerably, the practice of bishops' overseeing many dioceses was outlawed, and there was a new emphasis on the moral and intellectual quality of those training for the priesthood. The Catholic Reformation also witnessed a flowering of spiritual and devotional writings: for example, St Teresa of Avila, who began a reform movement within the Carmelite order, produced a number of writings on prayer, and St John of the Cross, another Carmelite reformer, wrote his *Spanish Canticle*, a poem based on the biblical Song of Songs, using the imagery of a love affair to describe the relationship between Christ and the Church. The Holy Spirit, who brings about this spiritual union, fuels this intimate relationship. According to Edward Howells, these two saints represent 'the culmination of the rich medieval development of Christian mystical theology in western Europe'.[44]

THE EVANGELICAL AWAKENINGS

The stories of the great revivals of the 18th and 19th centuries have been well documented and make for inspiring reading.[45] What stands out from these 'great awakenings' is not simply the fact that hundreds of thousands of people were won for Christ across the world, but that God did it through the preaching of his Word and the outpouring of his Spirit. We can see this by focusing on the three most well-known figures of the first Great Awakening (1727–50), before moving on to some of the key figures of 19th-century awakenings.

Jonathan Edwards has been described as 'one of those re-markable eighteenth century people who combined the best of Enlightenment intellectualism with the most earnest Christian zeal... a brilliant man, one of the most original theologians to be born in North America'.[46] He was an orthodox and committed Calvinist, passionate about teaching the Bible and preaching the gospel, and, while working as pastor of a church in Massachusetts, found himself overseeing 'a surprising work of God', as he called it.[47] In the autumn of 1734 he had started to preach with a passion to bring about conversions, and by December of that year 'the Spirit of God began extraordinarily to set in and wonderfully to work among us,' as he later wrote. Towns and Porter describe the effect of his ministry with succinct clarity:

As the Spirit of God worked through the preaching of the Scriptures, people responded in various ways. Some wept out of deep sorrow and distress as they became convinced of their sin. Others rejoiced in the joy of their salvation, overwhelmed with a new love for the brethren. Still others agonised in prayer for unconverted friends and loved ones. There was a deep sense of the presence of God in their midst.[48]

These are precisely the manifestations that Edwards himself de-scribes in great detail in his *Surprising Work*, for he was a keen observer of spiritual experiences. This was further developed in three major treatises: *The Distinguishing Marks of the Work of the Spirit of God* (1741), *Some Thoughts on the Revival of Religion in New England* (1742), and his masterpiece on religious experience, *A Treatise Concerning Religious Affections* (1746). Caldwell and Sweeney give us a brilliant summary of his balanced views:

When the Holy Spirit works saving grace into an individual, Edwards argued, his work is always accompanied by a change in the person's affections. The soul intimately feels the divine truths that it beholds: just prior to conversion it knows the terror of what it is to be under the just wrath of God, and upon trusting Christ it is overjoyed at the beauty, glory and grace of God revealed in the Gospel. Thus true Christianity is not simply an affair of morality but a loving communion with the sovereign creator. Yet true grace in the soul never bypasses the need for holy living or the church, but will always tend towards certain patterns of behaviour: true humility before God, a deep love for Christ, a holy life and a respect for the order established in the community of faith. These alone are the true signs of a converted life.[49]

George Whitefield was a companion and fellow worker with Edwards in the American colonies, but he was also a co-worker with John Wesley in England, Scotland and Wales. He was another strong Calvinist whose life's work was focused on fulfilling the great commission. Having experienced spiritual new birth while a young man at Oxford University, he was filled with a fire to preach it to others, both indoors and outdoors, in chapels and fields, to aristocracy and to miners. He was an exceptionally gifted speaker who used his acting and oratorical training to preach the good news of Christ, and vast crowds came to hear him. When he and Edwards were ministering in America (1740–41), thousands came to faith and many new churches were established as revival spread south into New England and Virginia. One church leader observed, 'Our lectures flourish, our Sabbaths are joyous, our churches increase and our ministers have new life and spirit in their work.'[50]

Subsequent generations have judged Whitefield to be the best known evangelist of the 18th century and one of the greatest itinerant preachers in the history of Protestantism.[51] Professor Gerald Cragg describes him as 'a preacher of extraordinary power' whose sermons 'produced dramatic results'.[52] Wherein lay the secret of this power? Surely it is found in the promise of Jesus that is intricately attached to the great commission that became the focus of Whitefield's life: 'You will receive power when the Holy Spirit comes on you; and you will be my witnesses... to the ends of the earth' (Acts 1:8–9). His was a particularly special anointing.

John Wesley had a nominal Christian faith until his well-known experience of Christ in a Moravian chapel in London when he felt his heart 'strangely warmed'. From then on, he only wanted to do one thing. He dedicated himself to preaching the gospel of Christ to those who hadn't heard it: 'In churches and churchyards, on village greens, in fields and in natural amphitheatres, he proclaimed the gospel and "offered Christ" to the vast crowds that gathered to listened to him. All the time his message was the Bible, for he knew that its overriding purpose was to point to Christ.'[53] His sermons were well reasoned and heavily doctrinal, but they managed to hold the rapt attention of his hearers. More importantly, they produced some extraordinary results. As he recorded in his journal, 'While I was preaching, one before me dropped down as dead, and presently a second or a third. Five others sank down in half an hour, most of whom were in violent agonies. We called upon the Lord and he gave us an answer of peace.'[54] No wonder Gerald Cragg also describes John Wesley as 'a preacher of extraordinary power'.[55] In all, he travelled 250,000 miles in the UK alone, and preached 40,000 sermons.

But Wesley's preaching of Christ was undergirded by a theology of the Spirit from start to finish. For him, God's grace was almost synonymous with the work of the Holy Spirit. God's sovereign plan of salvation was a process of the Spirit's work in three stages: firstly, prevenient grace, which is the work of God's Spirit in the lives of people between conception and conversion, initiating a longing to seek after God; secondly, justifying grace, which is the Holy Spirit's work in bringing about regeneration and imputing righteousness to the believer; and thirdly, sanctifying grace, which is the work that happens between conversion and death, making us holy and preparing us for heaven.[56] Just as there was no salvation without Christ, there was no experience of salvation without the Holy Spirit, according to Wesley.

The Evangelical awakenings of the 18th century blossomed under the proclamation of the Word of God and the outpouring of the Spirit of God, as did further revivals during the 19th century, such as the one in New England in 1830, overseen by the evangelist Charles Finney. Previously a lawyer, he used his logical mind and oratorical skills to press home the gospel in Rochester, New York, and thousands responded. The Rochester revival sparked further revivals all over New England, and one estimate made by a respected preacher, Lyman Beecher, was that 100,000 commitments to Christ were made in that single year. What was the secret of this extraordinary evangelist? Church historians cite an experience of anointing which it is best to let him describe in his own words:

The Holy Spirit descended upon me in a manner that seemed to go through me, body and soul. I could feel the impression, like a wave of electricity, going through and through me. Indeed it seemed to come in waves and waves of liquid love... It seemed like the very breath of God... I wept aloud with joy and love... These waves came over me, and over me, and over me, one after the other, until I recollect I cried out, 'I shall die if these waves continue to pass over me.' I said, 'Lord, I cannot bear any more.' [57]

A similar experience happened about 30 years later to another American preacher, D.L. Moody, whose evangelistic campaigns shook England and America in the 1870s and 1880s, and the significance of his ministry is captured by his biographer, Lyle Dorsett:

At least a hundred million people heard him preach; millions professed faith in Christ for the first time; countless souls returned to faith after drifting away; and millions more had their faith and ministry encouraged by his messages... No one in the nineteenth century did more than Moody to reach non-Christians, make disciples, train a new generation of home and foreign workers and encourage others to commit their lives to gospel ministry.[58]

What was the secret of his effectiveness? It was two faithful women, sitting on the front row of his church, praying for him to know 'the power of the Spirit' on his preaching. He became increasingly aware of his need to know this anointing, and began to seek the Lord over several months. In his own words:

I was crying all the time that God would fill me with his Spirit. Well, one day, in the city of New York—oh what a day!—I cannot describe it. I seldom refer to it; it is almost too sacred an experience to name... I can only say that God revealed himself to me, and I had such an experience of his love that I had to ask him to stay his hand. I went to preaching again. The sermons were not different; I did not present any new truths, yet hundreds were converted. I would not now be placed back where I was before that blessed experience if you should give me all the world.'[59]

Lyle Dorsett makes an extremely telling observation about this: 'In the wake of this powerful experience, Moody's ministry became astoundingly effective.'[60]

We can't leave the 19th century without mentioning C.H. Spurgeon (1834–92), unquestionably the finest preacher of his time and, some would argue, the best preacher in the history of the Church.[61] The well-known theologian and pastor Helmut Thielicke said, 'Sell all [the books] you have... and buy Spurgeon.'[62] He was a staunch Calvinist and a true heir of Puritan spirituality, believing that the evangelical movement of his day needed to recover three aspects of the Puritans: their rigorous theology, warm spirituality and down-to-earth practicality. But he was also acutely aware of the need for the power and anointing of the Holy Spirit on the pulpits up and down the country. Here is what he said in a sermon at New Park Street Chapel, Southwark, in 1855, entitled 'The power of the Holy Ghost':

There are diversities of operations; and during the last few years it has been the case that the diversified operations have consisted in very little pouring out of the Spirit. Ministers have gone on in dull routine, continually preaching—preaching—preaching, and little good has been done. I do hope that perhaps a fresh era has dawned upon us, and that there is a better pouring out of the Spirit even now. For the hour is coming, and it may be even now is, when the Holy Ghost shall be poured out again in such a wonderful manner, that many shall run to and fro, and knowledge shall be increased—the knowledge of the Lord shall cover the earth as the waters cover the surface of the great deep; when his kingdom shall come, and his will shall be done on earth even as it is in heaven. [63]

Before we move from this period, it is worth remembering that, in addition to the vast number of people won for Christ, there were two other blessings of these revivals. Firstly, there was the birth of world missions, with the founding of many mission societies and the ministries of William Carey, Hudson Taylor, David Livingstone, C.T. Studd, Mary Slessor and Henry Martyn, among others. Secondly, there was a great movement from Evangelicism towards social reform under the godly leadership of such figures as William Wilberforce, Lord Shaftesbury, William and Catherine Booth, George Muller, Elizabeth Fry and Thomas Barnardo. The proclaiming of the biblical Christ in the power of the Holy Spirit not only had an extraordinary impact on the world but also affected every area of society. Spurgeon's longings were being fulfilled even as he spoke. [64]

THE 20TH CENTURY

The last century was a momentous period in terms of both international affairs and religious movements, and space does not allow us to attempt to tell the story. It has been well documented by church historians, and their studies deserve our careful study.

However, in order to set the scene for an examination of some of the key figures within Evangelicalism, Patrick Johnstone, author of the international church prayer guide *Operation World* (2001 edition), has summarised the trends in international church growth during the last 100 years. Firstly, there has been massive growth of the church in the continents of Africa, Asia and Latin America, in marked contrast to the decline in Europe and North America. Secondly, the number of evangelicals worldwide has expanded enormously, from 84.5 million in 1960 to 420 million in 2000. Thirdly, the astonishing spread of Pentecostalism, from almost nothing at the beginning of the century to 116 million in 2000, has made it the fastest-growing movement within Christianity. Fourthly, following on from this, the huge impact of Charismatic renewal on all the established denominations (including Catholic and Orthodox) has been undeniable, with the worldwide appeal of the Alpha Course being just one indication. Fifthly, the church has not only survived but is now thriving in countries where it was being persecuted, most notably in Russia, China, India, Ethiopia, Sudan, Korea and a number of Muslim states. There are, of course, other, more concerning trends that we can't ignore, but those five are really something to celebrate.

I have chosen to give an historical perspective on the partnership of Word and Spirit through the ministries of four leaders within English-speaking Evangelicalism during the past 50 years. I have chosen these four for two reasons: firstly, I believe they have significantly raised the profile of the ministry of the Word or the ministry of the Spirit or both; and secondly, they have been people who have had an impact on my own life through their ministries, so I can talk about them with a degree of personal reflection, not just out of research done from history books.

I want to begin with the man to whom I owe more than to any other Christian leader. I began to devour John Stott's writings as an undergraduate, and then had the privilege of hearing him preach seven nights in a row at the 1977 Christian Union mission in Cambridge. The clarity of his preaching, the strength of his convictions, his faithfulness to the task of biblical exposition, his passion for evangelism and his personal warmth and humility left a lasting impression on me, as they did on many of my contemporaries. Professor Alister McGrath has suggested that the growth of post-war English Evangelicalism was attributable more to Stott than any other person; he 'became a role model for a younger generation of ordinands in England'.[65] The historian Adrian Hastings goes even further and says that Stott became 'one of the most influential figures in the Christian world', who was 'the recognised senior theologian and thinker of world evangelicalism'.[66] As the years have gone by, there are two aspects of his ministerial career that have continued to help and resource me in my ministry. Firstly, there are his very fine commentaries on the Bible, scholarly and well researched, but written with pastors and preachers in mind. I was also inspired by his masterly book *I Believe in Preaching*, published in the year of my ordination. The other aspect has been his ecumenical generosity of spirit towards all orthodox Christians and his desire to hold together the different shades of Evangelicalism and celebrate what they have in common. In his personal plea for unity, *Evangelical Truth*, he writes comprehensively about the ministry of the Holy Spirit in Chapter 3, but the chapter is introduced as follows:

The twentieth century has witnessed an unfortunate disagreement among evangelical Christians about the work of the Holy Spirit... on the one hand, there is recognition that Pentecostalism is the fastest-growing Christian movement in the world, providing abundant evidence of God's blessing upon it. On the other hand there is genuine anxiety that it is often growth without depth, so there is much super-ficiality everywhere. My personal conviction is that what unites us is considerably greater than what divides us, and my concern in this chapter is to concentrate on the former while not concealing the latter.[67]

Jeffrey Greenman talks in a similar vein about Stott's theology being balanced and measured, inclusive of the range of biblical perspectives: '[It] expressed a cross-centred, deeply Trinitarian form of classical evangelical faith and constantly exemplified a perspective he liked to call "balanced, biblical Christianity" ("BBC"), bringing together in harmony concerns that too often are opposed: personal and corporate, inward and outward, prayer and action, evangelism and social concern, word and Spirit, boldness and compassion'.[68] John Stott's biographer, Timothy Dudley-Smith, formerly Bishop of Thetford, said that he exemplified the essential marks of Evangelicalism: 'the search for holiness, the spread of the gospel and the cross of Christ; underpinned of course in all true Evangelicalism by the word of the Scriptures and the work of the Spirit'.[69]

The next leader I have chosen is David Watson, best known as the gracious and gifted minister of St Michael le Belfry in York, under whose leadership the church grew into a centre for evangelism and renewal; and also as the international evangelist who conducted 58 missions in five continents between 1978 and 1983, and was responsible for leading hundreds of people to Christ. When I heard him speak, I was riveted by his relaxed warmth, compelling clarity and persuasive presentation of the gospel. However, there were two other ways in which his ministry had an impact on me, in addition to his evangelism. Firstly, I was enormously helped by his books, especially *I Believe in the Church, I Believe in Evangelism,* and *Discipleship*. There was endless sermon material here; but more than that, there was a vision of how to develop a lively, growing church which greatly inspired me as an emerging church leader. Michael Green wrote in the foreword to *I Believe in the Church*:

[David] has rediscovered the dying art of church building: not in bricks and mortar, but in lives. He has seen a remarkable work grow under his hand during the past twelve years or so. It is a church where the leadership is shared, where prayer is central, where the sacraments are dynamic, where art and drama and dance adorn the worship. A church where the gifts of the Spirit mingle with his graces of character... It is a church which has learnt the pastoral value of the small group, the renewing power of the Holy Spirit, the mutual caring of members for one another... It seeks to go back to the New Testament.[70]

I found myself praying, 'Lord, please use me to build churches like that'!

Secondly, I saw in David Watson an integration of Word and Spirit. He was not only a gifted preacher and evangelist, but he was also an architect of church community, allowing the Holy Spirit to minister in and through the body of Christ by the use of spiritual gifts. He wrote movingly in his autobiography about his gratitude to his Conservative Evangelical nurturing, which introduced him to Christ and gave him a love of the Bible and a passion for evangelism,[71] and his growing openness to Charismatic renewal resulting from his closer study of the New Testament, which gave him a fresh joy and intimacy in his relationship with God, and fresh power and vision for the work of the kingdom.[72]

My third figure is Jim Packer. I read his *Knowing God* while I was an undergraduate, and I am still feeling the effects of it. His writings, including *God Has Spoken* and *Evangelism and the Sovereignty of God*, gave me a systematic theology that undergirded my Christian experience. Formerly Professor of Historical and Systematic Theology at Regent College, Vancouver, he is a staunch Calvinist, for whom Reformed Christianity is 'evangelicalism in its purest form'.[73] J.P. Greenman describes him as 'among the most influential figures in English-speaking evangelicalism during the latter half of the twentieth century... the professional theologian most widely and popularly accepted, someone to whom the evangelical movement frequently looked for insight and guidance'.[74]

Some might feel it is appropriate to describe him only as a theologian of the Word, given his Reformed credentials, but I am not so sure. I recently reread *Keep in Step with the Spirit* and two things struck me forcefully. Firstly, there is his well-rounded and Christocentric theology of the Holy Spirit, grounded in the Scriptures, no doubt influenced by the Puritans, and earthed in the life and experience of the believer. Packer believed that all true theology should be applied into our experience; knowing it in our heads is not good enough. Charismatics, surely, can warm to such practical and applied theology. Secondly, he is affirming of many aspects of the Charismatic movement, while being critical when Scripture demands it. Having explained that the Bible gives us two ways of testing any movement of spiritual renewal (the creedal test and the moral test), he then concludes:

When we apply these two tests to the Charismatic movement, it becomes plain at once that God is in it... Its main effect everywhere is to promote robust Trinitarian faith, personal fellowship with the divine Saviour and Lord whom we meet in the New Testament, repentance, obedience, and love to fellow Christians, expressed in ministry of all sorts towards them—plus a zeal for evangelistic outreach that puts the staider sort of churchman to shame.[75]

He then affirms in more detail what he sees as the positive blessings of the movement, before highlighting the potential pitfalls. But the overall tone is decidedly positive and of a bridge-building nature.

My fourth and final figure, Michael Green, refuses to retire from the Lord's work despite being in his 80s (there have been at least three failed attempts to help him!). He continues to lead parish and university missions and to train the future leaders of the church. Affectionately known as the 'English Billy Graham', it ought to be remembered that he was also the Rector of St Aldates, Oxford; the Principal of St John's College, Nottingham; Professor of Evangelism at Regent College, Vancouver; and one of the Archbishop of Canterbury's Springboard Team on Evangelism.

What has been Michael's enduring legacy to the church at large? I would suggest three major contributions: firstly, his commitment to evangelism as the Church's highest priority, which has inspired a whole generation of church leaders; secondly, his brilliant apologetics for the Christian faith, arising out of a rigorous biblical theology; and thirdly, his gracious welcome, and critique, of the Charismatic movement in the light of the Bible's teaching.[76] Some years after writing *I Believe in the Holy Spirit*, he was even more overt in his advocacy of the partnership of Word and Spirit:

The Spirit and the Word are friends, not foes. It is therefore tragic to see charismatics and evangelicals in tension with one another on this issue. Charismatics should be saying, 'Back to Scripture. Get thrilled with it. Obey it. Test all claims by it.' Evangelicals, for their part, should be saying, 'Let us not be satisfied until we see vital Christianity in our church, the gifts of the Spirit as well as his fruit.' They belong together.[77]

Michael has never lost his conviction in the authority and sufficiency of the Scriptures, however: he was the guest speaker at a 'Mere Anglicanism' conference in South Carolina, in 2008, speaking on the subject 'Scripture—Revelation or Speculation?', and in closing he issued this challenge to preachers:

Finally, the preachers among us do need to learn to expound the scriptures… Our job is not to use a text of scripture as a springboard for our own ideas, but to allow the text to impact the hearers with the greatest clarity and force. We are to be servants of the Word, breaking it up into bite-sized portions so that people can understand its meaning and context and can apply it to their own lives… It is an area we need to work at if we really believe that scripture is God's revelation, not mere human speculation.[78]

There have, of course, been many other leading figures within the Evangelical movement whom God has used to build his kingdom: Dick Lucas and David Jackman and the training of Bible teachers through the Proclamation Trust and the Cornhill Training

Course; David Pytches and John Coles and their leadership of the thriving New Wine movement; Nicky Gumbel and Rico Tice, the inspirations behind the Alpha Course and Christianity Explored respectively; the evangelical scholarship of F.F. Bruce, Howard Marshall, Chris Wright, Don Carson, Tom Wright, Gordon Fee, Alister McGrath and others; Steven Croft, Graham Cray and Mike Moynagh and the whole movement for Mission-Shaped Church and Fresh Expressions—and these are only the tip of an iceberg.

As already mentioned, however, I chose these four—Stott, Watson, Packer and Green—because they have a particular relevance to the subject of this book. All four call us to a deep loyalty to the Bible, a discerning openness to the Spirit and a deep passion for the honour and glory of Christ. As we move into the second decade of the 21st century and the tribes of Evangelicalism grow stronger but, at the same time, more separated, we would do well to listen to their wisdom and rebuild those bridges of love, trust and mutual respect.

CONCLUSION

We have now leapfrogged through 4000 years of biblical and church history, and have noticed a recurring theme, like a musical symphony that has a beautiful melody emerging at all the important moments. Let me try again to describe the melody so that we can capture the salient lessons for leadership in the church today.

1) The ministries of the Word and the Spirit are intimately connected

The image of a good marriage comes to mind: what makes it good? Not that two individuals get subsumed into each other and lose their fundamental personalities, and not that two people operate completely independently as if their marriage meant nothing and it didn't matter that they had joined themselves into a new family unit. No, a good marriage is one where both individuals thrive and develop, becoming all that they were meant to be, because there is an atmosphere of warmth and love and trust. This blossoming of personality is never at the expense of the other, for the couple are one unit, joined in heart and mind for the common purpose of being a family. A divorce would be a heartbreaking tragedy.

The same is true of the marriage of Word and Spirit. God's intention, which I have tried to show, is that he has joined them together in his redemptive purposes for the whole of eternity. This does not mean that their identities have been merged into each other, for the Spirit is not the Word, and the Word is not the Spirit. They retain distinguishable identities as sacred scripture and sovereign God. So, while it is true that the ministry of the Word *is* the ministry of the Spirit (what else could it be?),[79] this is only part (but a vital part) of the biblical theology of the Spirit's work, as we have seen.[80]

Nor does it mean that the Word and the Spirit operate completely separately, as if they had never been joined. It should trouble us when the Word is preached and then the leader of the service says, 'We now welcome the Holy Spirit!' Wasn't the Holy Spirit involved in the preaching (not to mention the preparation)? Surely the Holy Spirit should be welcomed at the beginning of the service, invited to teach us at the opening of God's Word, and given permission to work deeply in us by way of response. Similarly, it should concern us when the Word is opened without any reference to the Holy Spirit. Can we understand what God is saying to us without the Spirit's enlightenment? Won't the Holy Spirit be prompting a response and calling us to a deeper obedience?

In the marriage of Word and Spirit, both have their separate identities and distinguishable ministries. And yet, as both ministries thrive, there is considerable overlap, for the ministry of the Word must involve the Spirit for it to be effective, and the ministry of the Spirit should always take us back to the Word for clarity, testing and deeper understanding. The blossoming of each ministry is never at the expense of the other, for they are not in competition. Instead, they work together in the common purpose of glorifying Christ, building up the Church and extending the kingdom. A divorce would be a heartbreaking tragedy.

2) The ministries of Word and Spirit are infinitely important

The reasons why they are so important now become clear. Firstly, God himself has joined them together and it is not for us to divide them. If we do divorce them in our churches, by exalting one to the exclusion of the other, then something sacred is ripped apart. Secondly, God has given us his Word and his Spirit as our two greatest resources for Christian ministry and mission. Do we want to see people coming to Christ? Do we want to build a Christian community? Do we want to preach with clarity and power? Do we want to give visionary leadership? Do we want to minister to the sick and the broken? Do we want to stay close to Christ amid all the demands of ministry? We will need the Word and the Spirit, for God has no other way. Thirdly, it is through the ministry of Word and Spirit that God commands his blessing. We saw this in our biblical survey and in our historical overview: periods of revival and renewal (such as the Great Awakenings) were periods when the Word of God was being preached and the Spirit of God was being poured out. It is a time of growth for the Church, change for society and healing for the nations, in anticipation of the glorious things to come.[81]

But what does this 'good marriage' look like in practice, in terms of Christian leadership of a local church? The rest of this book provides a model of gospel ministry that is resourced by the Word and the Spirit. For some at the early stages of preparation and training, I hope it will serve as a 'marriage preparation' course, giving you a vision of what could be. For others who are already happily committed to a Word and Spirit ministry, I hope it will serve as a 'marriage enrichment' course, encouraging you to press on with renewed hope and determination. To others, who may feel that the Word and the Spirit have become distanced from each other at some stage along the line, I hope it will serve as a 'marriage counselling' course, providing a way back into a close and intimate partnership again.

Notes

1 John Stott, *I Believe in Preaching* (Hodder and Stoughton, 1982), pp. 18–21

2 The Didache, in *Ante-Nicene Fathers*, Vol. VII (1886, Eerdmans 1975), p. 378

3 Justin Martyr, Chap. LXVII, in *Ante-Nicene Fathers*, Vol. I, p. 186

4 Tertullian, Chap. XXXIX, in *Ante-Nicene Fathers*, Vol. III, p. 46

5 Clyde E. Fant and William M. Pinson (eds.), *Twenty Centuries of Great Preaching* (Word, 1976), Vol. 1, pp. 108–9

6 Phillip Schaff (ed.), *The Nicene and Post-Nicene Fathers* Vol. IX (1892, Eerdmans 1975), p. 22

7 1 Clement 47:3; 13:1; Barnabas 9:2; 10:2

8 Simon Ponsonby, *God Inside Out* (Kingsway, 2007), p. 62

9 Professor Ronald Kydd has a study on this period in his *Charismatic Gifts in the Early Church* (Hendrickson, 1984) and finds that the gifts of the Spirit did not die out with the apostles. On the contrary, they remained very important to the church throughout the first and second centuries. 'The Church prior to AD200 was charismatic,' he concludes. But he also notes that 'there came a point around AD260 when they no longer fitted into the highly organised, well-educated, wealthy, socially powerful Christian communities. The Church did not lose its soul, but it did lose those special moments when God broke into the lives of men and women.'

10 A. Cleveland Coxe, *The Ante-Nicene Fathers*, Vol. 6 (Eerdmans, 1951), p. 190

11 *Against Heresies* (Book II, Chapter 32, paragraph 4). From *Ante-Nicene Fathers* Vol. 1, eds. Alexander Roberts, James Donaldson and A. Cleveland Coxe (Christian Literature Publishing Co., 1885)

12 Coxe, *Ante-Nicene Fathers*, Vol. 3, p. 107

13 Coxe, *Ante-Nicene Fathers*, Vol. 5, p. 641

14 See Jonathan Hill, *The New Lion Handbook: The History of Christianity* (Lion Hudson, 2007), chs. 3–8 or Tim Dowley (ed.), *The Monarch History of the Church* Vols. 2 and 3 (Monarch, 2005) or Owen Chadwick (ed.), *The Pelican History of the Church* Vol. 2.

15 Quoted in Alister McGrath, *An Introduction to Christianity* (Blackwell, 1997), p. 174

16 Joseph Defferari, *The Fathers of the Church* Vol. 24 (The Catholic University of America Press), pp. 431–445

17 Placid Hermann, *St Francis of Assisi* (Herald Press), pp. 59–60

18 Michael Mitton, *Restoring the Woven Cord: Strands of Celtic Christianity for the Church today* (BRF, 2010)

19 Gary Badcock captures this perfectly: 'The spirituality of the Reformation, by which the divine presence is discovered and expressed and lived with, is above all a spirituality of the Word, a spirituality that has the Bible at its centre and in a very real sense at its heart. That one encounters God here, distinctly and authentically, in the simple reading or preaching or hearing of the text, constitutes the great burden of the Reformation approach...' (*Light of Truth and Fire of Love*, Erdmanns, 1997), p. 88.

20 Quoted in Hill, *New Lion Handbook: History of Christianity*, p. 252

21 Martin Luther, 'A Prelude on the Babylonian Captivity of the Church' in E.G. Rupp, *Luther's Progress to the Diet of Worms 1521* (SCM, 1951), pp. 85–86

22 Luther, 'A Prelude', in Rupp, *Luther's Progress*

23 Martin Luther, 'Of the Liberty of a Christian Man' in Rupp, *Luther's Progress*

24 Theodore Tappert (ed. nd.), *Luther: Letters of Spiritual Counsel*, The Library of Christian Classics (Westminster Press) Vol. 18, p. 52

25 See Stanley Burgess, *The New International Dictionary of Pentecostal and Charismatic Movements* (Zondervan, 2003)

26 Alasdair Heron, *The Holy Spirit* (Marshall Morgan and Scott, 1983), p. 105

27 Martin Luther, 'A Simple Way to Pray', *Luther's Works*, Vol. 43, p. 198

28 W.S. Reid, article on Calvin in Walter Elwell (ed.), *Evangelical Dictionary of Theology* (Marshall Pickering, 1984), p. 185

29 John Calvin, *Institutes* Vol. 4.1.9, p. 1023

30 Brian Gaybba, *The Spirit of Love* (Geoffrey Chapman Theological Library, 1987), pp. 98–99

31 'Testimonium Spiritus Sancti Internum' in J. McNeill (ed.), *Calvin: Institutes of Christian Religion* (Westminster Press, 1960) 1.7.4

32 Calvin, *Institutes*, pp. 16–17

33 Documented by Jack Deare in *Surprised by the Voice of God* (Kingsway, 1996), pp. 69–86

34 Henry Baird, *The Huguenots* (Charles Scribner, 1895) Vol. 2, pp. 186–187

35 Paul Helm, *Calvin: A Guide for the Perplexed* (T&T Clark, 2008), p. 125

36 Mark Noll, 'Puritanism' in Elwell, *Evangelical Dictionary of Theology*, p. 898

37 Irvonwy Morgan, *The Godly Preachers of the Reformation Settlement* (Epworth, 1965), pp. 10–11

38 Richard Baxter, *The Reformed Pastor* (1656, Epworth 2nd edition 1950), p. 75

39 Ponsonby, *God Inside Out*, ch. 15

40 John Owen, 'The Work of the Spirit' in Goold (ed.), *Works of John Owen* Vol. 4

41 Geoffrey Nuttall, *The Holy Spirit in Puritan Faith and Experience* (Chicago, 1992), p. 23

42 Owen Chadwick, *The Reformation* (Penguin, 1964), pp. 180–182

43 Ponsonby, *God Inside Out*, p. 297

44 Edward Howells, 'A new spirituality: the Carmelite mystics' in *The History of Christianity* (Lion, 2007), p. 260

45 See, for example, E. Towns and D. Porter, *The Ten Greatest Revivals Ever* (Vine, 2000), chs. 2–5 or Hill, *The New Lion History of Christianity*, pp. 324–352

46 Hill, *The New Lion History of Christianity*, p. 329

47 *A Faithful Narrative of the Surprising Work of God* (1737)

48 Towns and Porter, *Ten Greatest Revivals Ever*, pp. 62–63

49 R. Caldwell and D. Sweeney, 'Jonathan Edwards' in *Biographical Dictionary of Evangelicals* (IVP, 2003), pp. 201–205

50 Quoted in Geoffrey Hanks, *Seventy Great Christians* (Christian Focus, 1992), p. 169

51 See, for example, M. Noll, 'George Whitefield' in Elwell, *Evangelical Dictionary of Theology*, pp. 1170–1171

52 Gerald Cragg, *The Church and the Age of Reason* (Penguin, reprinted 1984), p. 144

53 John Stott, *I Believe in Preaching* (Hodder, 1982), pp. 31–32

54 Recorded in Cragg, *Church and the Age of Reason*, p. 144

55 Cragg, *Church and the Age of Reason*, p. 144

56 For a fuller treatment of Wesley's theology of the Holy Spirit, see 'John Wesley' and 'The Wesley Tradition' in Elwell, *Evangelical Dictionary of Theology*, pp. 1163–1167

57 Bernard A. Weisberger, *They Gathered at the River* (Little, Brown, 1958), p. 92

58 L.W. Dorsett, 'D.L. Moody' in *Biographical Dictionary of Evangelicals*, pp. 433–437

59 D.L. Moody, *Secret Power* (Regal, 1987, originally published 1881), p. 17

60 Moody, *Secret Power*, p. 436

61 See J. Armstrong, 'C.H. Spurgeon' in *Biographical Dictionary of Evangelicals*, p. 626

62 Quoted by Armstrong, *Biographical Dictionary of Evangelicals*, p. 626

63 www.spurgeon.org/sermons/0030.htm. I recommend reading the whole sermon. Here Spurgeon was not downplaying the task of preaching but was emphasising the fact that preaching without the power of the Holy Spirit achieves very little, if anything at all. He was longing to see a new wave of the Spirit's outpouring upon the preaching ministry that would usher in 'the latter-day glory'.

64 See David Bebbington's summary of the achievement of the Evangelical movement in the 19th century in *Evangelicalism in Modern Britain* (Unwin Hyman, 1989), p. 149

65 Quoted in J.P. Greenman, 'J.R.W. Stott' in *Biographical Dictionary of Evangelicals*, pp. 639–640

66 Quoted in *Biographical Dictionary of Evangelicals*, p. 641

67 John Stott, *Evangelical Truth* (IVP, 1999), p. 104

68 Stott, *Evangelical Truth*, p. 641

69 Quoted in Roger Steer, *Church on Fire* (Hodder, 1998), p. 454

70 David Watson, *I Believe in the Church* (Hodder and Stoughton, 1978), pp. 7–8

71 David Watson, *You Are My God* (Hodder and Stoughton, 1983) chs. 1–3

72 Watson, *You Are My God*, chs. 4–6

73 J.P. Greenman, 'J.I. Packer' in *Biographical Dictionary of Evangelicals*, p. 500

74 *Biographical Dictionary of Evangelicals*, p. 500

75 J.I. Packer, *Keep in Step with the Spirit* (IVP, 1984), p. 185

76 What Michael Green wrote in the Preface of *I Believe in the Holy Spirit* (Hodder and Stoughton, 1974) displays this openness and honesty: 'During the past 15 years I have had the privilege of living in a Christian community where the charismatic question has been a very live issue, and where "charismatic" and "non-charismatic" Christians have lived together in a high degree of mutual love and trust. It cannot be denied that the charismatic movement has in places brought division and suspicion. It is my conviction, and my experience, that this need not be so, and that the Spirit of unity would have it otherwise' (p. 8).

77 Michael Green, *Evangelism through the Early Church* (Hodder and Stoughton, 1990), p. 389

78 For a full text of his outstanding address, visit www.virtueonline.org

79 Ephesians 6:17

80 See Chapter 2

81 Revelation 21:1—22:6

LEADERSHIP
IMPLICATIONS

PREACHING AND TEACHING
THE BIBLE

Have you ever nodded off in a sermon? One of the world's worst preachers is reckoned to have been Dr Robert South, who, in 1689, is said to have put his entire congregation to sleep, including the king of England. At one point during his tedious monologue, he broke off to rebuke one of the congregation: 'Lord Lauderdale, rouse yourself!' he commanded. 'You snore so loudly you will wake the King'![1] The enormous irony of this amusing (and yet sad) story is that preaching is meant to wake people up, not put them to sleep. Preaching has been defined as 'thirty minutes in which to wake the dead'.[2]

Despite the popular perception, there is still a demand for good preaching. *The Times* ran an article on 19 January 2010 by Ruth Gledhill, Religion Correspondent, and Chris Smyth, entitled, 'To some, sermonising is a sin, but Christians still value the preacher'. It was based on a recent survey carried out by Durham's Codec research centre to mark the 50th anniversary of the College of Preachers. It stated:

Sermons, history shows, can be among the most revolutionary forms of human speech. From John Calvin to Billy Graham, preaching has had the power to topple princes, to set nation against nation, to inspire campaigners to change the world and impel people to begin life anew. In many churches this most vibrant of moments has withered to little more than 20 minutes of tired droning that serves only to pad out the gap between hymns and lunch. Yet some ember still seems to burn in Britain's 3.6 million regular churchgoers, for almost all of them feel a sense of expectation for the Sunday sermon, according to researchers at Durham University. Fully 96.6 per cent of those surveyed 'look forward' to the sermon, with 60 per cent saying it gave them a sense of God's love... The College of Preachers of Durham University admits that the results are 'counter-intuitive'—particularly in an age where 'sermonising' is seen as a deadly sin... Dr Rowan Williams, who as Archbishop of Canterbury is patron of the College of Preachers, is among the church leaders who have signed the college's jubilee pledge. This commits them to 'forward-looking preaching, engaging faithfully with the Bible, directly with the congregation and prophetically with the world, to proclaim Jesus as Lord'.[3]

THE IMPORTANCE OF PREACHING

Preaching and teaching the Bible is placed here deliberately at the start of the list of tasks for a Christian leader. The reasons for this should already be clear from our biblical and historical surveys: firstly, the New Testament writings (particularly the Pastoral Epistles) identify this task as being supremely important; secondly, this task is the primary way in which God has revealed himself to his people and continues to do so today. Furthermore, through the preaching of God's Word, God's people are fed and nourished, trained in godly living and equipped for Christian service. Preaching the gospel is also the primary way that people hear about and respond to the good news of Christ, and finally, teaching the Bible keeps the church anchored to the apostolic faith and guards against error and heresy. These are the theological foundations that undergird and shape a preaching ministry, and I don't know how anyone has the confidence to get into the pulpit who does not have them in place. John Stott has put it brilliantly: 'The essential secret [of effective preaching] is not mastering certain techniques but being mastered by certain convictions.'[4] Michael Quicke, Professor of Preaching and Communication at Northern Seminary, USA, has written passionately about the need for thinking about Christian leadership to include the central importance of preaching: 'Christian leadership belongs to preaching and preaching belongs to leadership because God's preachers are inevitably also his leaders.'[5]

The importance of preaching cannot be overstated. If we listen to some of the most influential Christian leaders of our generation, there is a powerful unanimity on the need for faithful biblical preaching. Martyn Lloyd-Jones, for example, who for 30 years was the minister of Westminster Chapel in London (1938–68) and is reckoned to have been the most powerful British preacher of the 1950s and '60s,[6] wrote in his classic *Preaching and Preachers*, 'The work of preaching is the highest and the greatest and the most glorious calling to which anyone can ever be called... the most urgent need in the Christian Church today is true preaching... it is obviously the greatest need of the world also.'[7]

John Stott, rejoicing in statistics of church growth but bemoaning the low standard of Christian living, believed that poor preaching of God's Word was largely responsible: 'To be sure, it is the Holy Spirit who renews the Church, but the Spirit's sword is the Word of God (Ephesians 6:17). Nothing, it seems to me, is more important for the life and growth, health and depth of the contemporary church than a recovery of serious biblical preaching.'[8]

Mark Stibbe, an internationally known Christian speaker and author, and until recently the Vicar of St Andrew's, Chorleywood, has written, 'Teaching is one of the most neglected spiritual gifts in the Body of Christ, particularly in Charismatic circles. It is for this reason that I am passionately committed to persuade, motivate and incite Christians, and particularly pastors and leaders, to start preaching and teaching with hearts on fire—to start expounding the Bible.'[9]

David Jackman, the former Director of the Cornhill Training Course, wrote an article calling for a rigorous study of God's Word to be at the heart of the training process for future Christian leaders: 'Where the Bible is properly preached and taught, God's voice is heard, sinners are saved, Christians develop in godliness and churches grow. The connection is not a coincidence.'[10] Greg

Haslam, one of Lloyd-Jones' successors at Westminster Chapel, and the general editor of the massive volume on preaching entitled *Preach the Word*, states, 'Christianity is an activity that expands *primarily* through the activity of preaching.'[11] Mike Pilavachi, the founder and leader of Soul Survivor and the pastor of Soul Survivor, Watford, writes about the need for inspired preaching to young people: 'More than anything we need to be authentic, passionate about what we are talking about and excited about the truth we have found. If we want our young people to get into the Word, we have to let them see that we passionately love this Book, and we do that by the way we teach it.'[12]

THE POWER OF PREACHING

To the powerful testimony of the Scriptures, church history and church leaders, let me add my own personal testimony from parish experience. I have constantly seen God at work through this ministry, not because I have been an exceptional preacher but because God's Word is exceptionally powerful. I have witnessed people's hearts being won and their lives changed. Let me give you just a very few examples. I remember a major building project being resourced by preaching through the book of Haggai. I recall a vision for Fresh Expressions of church being cast during a sermon series on the book of Acts. I was humbled to see God addressing gossip and backbiting through a series on the book of James. I noticed God challenging gambling habits in a series on 'Christian stewardship', and sexual promiscuity through a series on 1 and 2 Thessalonians. I was thrilled to see scientists and medics given hope by a biblical response to Richard Dawkins. I was encouraged to see homeless people engaging with Jesus through a sermon series at Café Church on Mark's Gospel. I witnessed people opening up to spiritual gifts through a series on 1 Corinthians 12—14. I noticed our worship reaching a new depth and quality after preaching on the Psalms. I saw new confidence in the uniqueness of Christ in our pluralistic society during a series on the 'I am' sayings in John's Gospel. I shall never forget the way God comforted the wounded members of our congregation through a sermon series on the chequered life story of Joseph.

So, despite its being intellectually challenging, emotionally exhausting and spiritually demanding, often involving burning candles at both ends, I believe in preaching more than ever. Nothing gives me greater excitement or deeper satisfaction than opening up a passage of Scripture, expounding it and applying it into the lives of my congregation—and then standing back and watching what God is doing. But I also know the power of preaching through being on the receiving end: God spoke powerfully to me through the Bible readings at New Wine in 2009 as Rich Nathan opened up the book of Proverbs, the team at St Aldates, Oxford (where we worship), never fail to bring a true and present word, and I am very privileged to hear two or three of our Wycliffe students preaching every week. I heard John Lennox, Professor of Mathematics at Oxford University, preach recently, and Christ won my heart all over again as John presented a robust Christian response to the new atheism.

Dick Lucas, previously the Rector of St Helen's, Bishopsgate, has had an enormous influence on the standard and quality of preaching in the UK and beyond. Many will be aware of his outstanding preaching ministry in the heart of the City of London. Even more significant, in terms of wider and longer-term influence, have been the training courses developing from his determination to see expository preaching in churches around the world. Peter Adam, Principal of Ridley College, Melbourne, captured something of the significance of Dick's influential ministry when he wrote:

Dick Lucas represents part of the great resurgence of Reformed expository preaching that has taken place in Great Britain after the Second World War. This resurgence was represented by Martyn Lloyd-Jones at Westminster Chapel, John Stott at All Souls, Langham Place, Dick Lucas at St Helen's, and William Still in Aberdeen... They were independent attempts to reassert the centrality and sufficiency of Scripture in the preaching of the church; they reflected the great expository preaching of Calvin in Geneva, and of Augustine and John Chrysostom in the early church.[13]

I was privileged to learn from Dick Lucas some of the essential principles of biblical preaching by watching him do it. Firstly, I learnt that God (not human beings) is the main subject of the Bible, and therefore we should approach every passage with the question, 'What does this teach us about God and his saving work through Christ?' Sermons are moments of divine self-revelation when God reveals himself to us again through his Word. They should reveal more of his greatness, goodness and grace. Secondly, using a golfing analogy, I learnt that we should 'let the club do the work'. By that I mean that the Bible has an authority and power of its own, and we don't have to try to do what the Bible itself can do. Our task as preachers is to do our homework and then let the Bible loose: to open up the text of Scripture, aware of its cultural and historical context and the original intention of the author(s), so that the original meaning becomes clear. The task of the preacher, then, is to bring this original meaning to his hearers and apply it with integrity and insight into their hearts and lives. God will do the rest, by his Spirit. Thirdly, I learnt that this ministry has to be my greatest priority in the week amid all the pressures and demands of parish ministry. This means getting to it early in the week, studying the text with the help of commentaries, reading round the subject, praying for wisdom and guidance, working hard at defining the main point and having a clear sense of direction, structuring it with clear points so that it is unmissable and memorable, and making appropriate and relevant application into the lives of people today. If the Bible is the spiritual food for our people, to help them grow up into Christ, then it is neglectful to them and dishonouring to God not to give it the priority it deserves.

John Stott wrote on his 70th birthday, 'Where are the Timothys of the next generation? Where are the young evangelical men and women, who are determined by God's grace to stand firm in Scripture... and who are committed to passing it on, as they give themselves to the ministry of conscientious exposition?'[14] It is important to note Stott's reference to 'men and women' in this call for expository preaching. This is not a task that should ever be seen as a male prerogative; women are not only called to it but also gifted for it. As my colleague, Revd Dr Liz Hoare (Tutor in Prayer and Spirituality at Wycliffe Hall), has pointed out:

At Pentecost God poured out his Spirit on all flesh, women and men together. I cannot help wondering that if the Church had maintained a better balance of Word and Spirit in its history, women's voices might not have been lost. They are certainly present in the New Testament and it is interesting that whenever there is renewal in the Church, women appear again. Notable examples are Hild in the early conversions of Northumbria, Julian during the flowering of English mysticism in the 14th century, the Puritan emphasis on the home, Quaker women preachers, early Methodist women preachers, the flourishing of overseas missions where women did pioneering work, and the modern Charismatic movement. Named and unnamed, women flourished at all levels of Christian community and the Church was blessed.[15]

The best sermon series on Ephesians that I have ever heard was given by one of my curates, the Revd Helen Marshall, and some of our finest preachers in training at Wycliffe Hall are women. Rosie Ward, one of the Church Pastoral Aid Society's Leadership Development Advisors, tackles the complex biblical texts around women in ministry in the opening chapter of her helpful book *Growing Women Leaders*, and she also gives us a brief biblical and historical overview of the ways in which God has used women through the centuries. Preaching is clearly one of them.[16]

THE SPIRIT IN PREACHING

We have already seen that the Holy Spirit is indispensible in helping us to study and understand the Bible: he inspired the biblical text, he illumines its meaning and he applies it into our hearts and lives.[17] So the preacher, in opening the Word of God, is entirely dependent on the Spirit of God for its effectiveness.[18] This has two consequences, one for the preacher and another for the sermon.

Firstly, as preachers, we should seek the anointing and empowering of the Holy Spirit. After all, Jesus was an anointed preacher[19] and the Spirit was poured out on the disciples at Pentecost precisely so that they could fulfil Jesus' great commission to preach the gospel to the ends of the earth.[20] Paul was very aware of the anointing of the Holy Spirit on his preaching in Thessalonica, in Corinth and in many other places too.[21]

C.H. Spurgeon, who has been called 'the Prince of Preachers', was well aware of this need for the empowering of the Holy Spirit:

However learned, godly and eloquent a minister may be, he is nothing without the Holy Spirit. The bell in the steeple may be well hung, fairly fashioned, and of the soundest metal, but it is dumb until the ringer makes it speak. And in like manner the preacher has no voice of quickening for the dead in sin, or comfort for living saints, until the divine spirit gives him a gracious pull, and bids him speak with power.[22]

In fact, each time he mounted the steps to the pulpit at the Metropolitan Tabernacle, where he regularly preached to between 6500 and 7000 people, he would say quietly to himself, 'I believe in the Holy Ghost. I believe in the Holy Ghost.'[23] He was practising what he preached!

Similarly, J.C. Ryle, the 19th-century evangelical Bishop of Liverpool, believed that the greatest need of his day was for an outpouring of the Holy Spirit upon the Church, and especially upon her preachers:

Pray daily for a great outpouring of the Spirit on the Church and on the world. This is the grand want of our day... The 'company of the preachers' in Christendom is far greater than it was in the days of St Paul; but the actual spiritual work done in the earth... is undoubtedly far less. We want more of the presence of the Holy Ghost—more in the pulpit, more in the congregation, more in the pastoral visit and more in the school. Where He is, there is life, health, growth and fruitfulness.[24]

Martyn Lloyd-Jones also urged preachers to seek the anointing of the Holy Spirit. In a very passionate and moving last chapter to his *Preaching and Preachers*, he firstly defines it:

It is the Holy Spirit falling on the preacher in a special manner. It is an access of power. It is God giving power, and enabling, through the Spirit, to the preacher in order that he may do this work in a manner that lifts it beyond the efforts of man to a position in which the preacher is being used by the Spirit and becomes the channel through which the Spirit works.

He then justifies it by many references to Scripture and church history, and concludes with an impassioned appeal to preachers: 'There is only one obvious conclusion. Seek Him! Seek Him! What can we do without Him? Seek Him! Seek Him always. But go beyond seeking Him; expect Him... This 'unction', this 'anointing', is the supreme thing. Seek it until you have it; be content with nothing less.'[25]

R.T. Kendall, another of Martyn Lloyd-Jones' successors at Westminster Chapel, speaks with great openness and vulnerability about his growing sense of needing the anointing of the Holy Spirit on his preaching ministry: 'I want more of the Holy Spirit than I want anything in the world... I have often said I wanted unction on my preaching, that I would push a peanut with my nose across London if that would bring it.'[26] David Holden, an international speaker for New Frontiers, put it succinctly: 'As much as my preaching needs to be truth, it needs the anointing of the Holy

Spirit.'[27] John Wesley once said, 'When you go out to preach, don't worry about how to gain an audience. Get on fire, and people will come to watch you burn.'[28]

Secondly, for each sermon, we should seek the wisdom and strength of the Holy Spirit. There is no part of the preaching process that does not involve him. He needs to be there in the preparation, so that while we study the commentaries and research the subject, we are praying, 'Lord, what do you want me to say? Holy Spirit, what do you want to teach? What do you want to accomplish in your kingdom purposes through this talk?' Then, the Spirit needs to be there in the delivery. John Piper talks openly about the way he disciplines himself to preach in the power and strength of the Holy Spirit: he admits his utter helplessness without the Spirit; he prays for help, power, humility and freedom; he trusts in specific Bible promises about God's help and strength; he acts in the confidence that God will fulfil his Word; and he is careful, at the end of his talk, to thank God for sustaining him to declare the truth of his Word.[29]

Finally, the Holy Spirit needs to be there in the response time, helping the people to receive the message that God has spoken and ministering his grace, strength or healing to them. I think we should not miss the opportunity to challenge people to be 'doers of the word, and not hearers only' and to remind them, 'Today, if you hear his voice, do not harden your hearts.'[30] It is worth noting that the writer of Hebrews says here in 3:7, 'As the Holy Spirit *says...*' (present tense), which implies an ongoing challenge to hear and obey the voice of God. I think it is wholly appropriate to give people a range of options at the end of the sermon. I would say, 'For some, you may need to go home, get on your knees in a quiet place and do business with God; for others, you may want to pray quietly in your seat, or ask someone sitting near you to pray with you. But for others, you may find it really helpful to come to the front of church and receive prayer from someone on our prayer ministry team.' This is not the time for hype or pressure, but it is the moment for real openness to the Holy Spirit, and a clear challenge to obey him. The real test of a sermon's effectiveness, however, is not the number of people who come forward but the number of lives changed in terms of a settled obedience to walk the way of the cross.

FIRE AND LIGHT IN THE PULPIT

Preaching, then, is a combination of the ministries of the Word and the Spirit. If we exalt the Spirit to the detriment of the Word, then God's truth is compromised and endangered. If we exalt the Word to the detriment of the Spirit, then God's power and illumination are lost. If, however, we allow the ministries of the Word and the Spirit to have their place in our preaching, then God's glory is revealed, God's truth is seen, God's gospel is received, God's people are built up and God's purposes are accomplished. What we need is fire and light in the pulpit, which is what C.H. Spurgeon was saying in the 19th century: 'There must be light as well as fire. Some preachers are all light and no fire, while others are all fire and no light. What we need is both fire and light.'[31] Richard Baxter, the Puritan preacher of the 17th century, spoke on similar lines: 'First light, then heat.'[32]

Perhaps Martyn Lloyd-Jones said it most powerfully. Here is his definition of preaching: 'What is preaching? Logic on fire! Eloquent reason! Are these contradictions? Of course they are not... It is theology on fire! And a theology which does not take fire, I maintain, is a defective theology... Preaching is theology coming through a man who is on fire!'[33]

Notes

1   Stephen Pile, *The Book of Heroic Failures* (Futura, 1979), p. 41

2   Greg Haslam (ed.), *Preach the Word!* (Sovereign World, 2006), p. 31

3   www.timesonline.co.uk/tol/comment/faith/article6993099.ece

4   John Stott, *I Believe in Preaching* (Hodder, 1982), p. 92

5   Michael Quicke, *360-Degree Leadership: Preaching to transform congregations* (Baker, 2006), p. 17

6   Quicke, *360-Degree Leadership*, p. 46

7   M. Lloyd-Jones, *Preaching and Preachers* (Hodder, 1971, p. 9

8   John Stott, *The Contemporary Christian* (IVP, 1992), p. 208

9   Haslam, *Preach the Word!* p. 65

10 Chris Green and David Jackman (eds.), *When God's Voice Is Heard* (IVP, 1995), p. 184

11 Haslam, *Preach the Word!* p. 35

12 Haslam, *Preach the Word!* p. 357

13 Green and Jackman, *When God's Voice Is Heard*, p. 28

14 Stott, *Contemporary Christian*, p. 172

15 Wycliffe Hall, July 2010

16 Rosie Ward, *Growing Women Leaders* (BRF, 2008), chs. 1–3

17 See page 42

18 Michael Quicke underlines the role of the Holy Spirit as being indispensible at every point in the preaching process: 'in the revealing, preaching, listening, and living. Minds, hearts, mouths, ears, individual lives, and communities are all within his influence' (*360-Degree Leadership*, p. 59).

19 Luke 4:14–19

20 Acts 1:8–9

21 1 Thessalonians 1:5; 1 Corinthians 2:4; Romans 15:18–19

22 Quoted in Haslam, *Preach the Word!* p. 437

23 Haslam, *Preach the Word!* pp. 248–249

24 J.C. Ryle, *Old Paths* (James Clark, 1977 edition), p. 290

25 Lloyd-Jones, *Preaching and Preachers*, p. 325

26 R.T. Kendal, *The Anointing* (Hodder, 1998), p. 13

27 Haslam, *Preach the Word!* p. 276

28 Quoted in Kendal, *The Anointing*, p. 88

29 John Piper, *The Supremacy of God in Preaching* (IVP, 1990), pp. 44–46

30 James 1:22 (RSV); Hebrews 3:7–8

31 C.H. Spurgeon, *The Soul Winner* (Pilgrim, 1978), p. 98

32 Quoted in Haslam, *Preach the Word!* p. 50

33 Lloyd-Jones, *Preaching and Preachers*, p. 97

DEVELOPING AND
IMPLEMENTING VISION

In 1997 I had the privilege of taking a sabbatical, and spent six weeks of it in the USA and Mexico looking at multicultural churches. The particular reason for looking at that subject was because I was vicar of a multicultural parish in inner-city Bristol and I needed to explore the issue in greater depth. One of the highlights of my trip was standing in the very place, at the top of the steps of the Lincoln Memorial in Washington DC, where Dr Martin Luther King Jr made his 'I have a dream' speech on 28 August 1963 in front of thousands of people who had gathered as part of a massive campaign for civil rights for black Americans.

In this speech he shared a moving and compelling vision of social and racial justice for the USA:

And so even though we face the difficulties of today and tomorrow, I still have a dream. It is a dream deeply rooted in the American dream. I have a dream that one day this nation will rise up and live out the true meaning of its creed: 'We hold these truths to be self-evident, that all men are created equal... I have a dream that my four little children will one day live in a nation where they will not be judged by the color of their skin but by the content of their character. I have a dream today![1]

This vision electrified the crowd and added fresh energy into a long and weary campaign. It was a vision that was deeply rooted in a biblical vision of the kingdom of God, which shouldn't surprise us because of King's Christian commitment as a Baptist pastor. Bill Hybels, in his book *Courageous Leadership*, comments on the lasting impact of this speech: 'Who can forget 1963? Dr Martin Luther King Jr painted a picture of a world without prejudice, hatred, or racism... Although Dr King was cruelly assassinated, his dream lives on. Almost forty years later his passion guides our nation as racial barriers fall.'[2]

This is the power of a vision. John Stott did a very similar thing at All Souls, Langham Place, on 24 November 1974, when the church was celebrating its 150th anniversary. He was asked by the staff to look into the future and share a vision of what God might do. He did it with due apologies to Martin Luther King!

I have a dream of a church that is a biblical church—which is loyal in every particular to the revelation of God in Scripture, whose pastors expound Scripture with integrity and relevance, and so seek to present every member mature in Christ, whose people love the Word of God, and adorn it with an obedient and Christ-like life, which is preserved from all unbiblical emphases, whose life manifests in the health and beauty of biblical balance. I have a dream of a biblical church.

I have a dream of a church that is a worshipping church—whose people come together to meet God and worship him, who know God is always in their midst and who bow down before him in great humility, who regularly frequent the table of the Lord Jesus, to celebrate his mighty act of redemption on the cross, who enrich the worship with their musical skills, who believe in prayer and lay hold of God in prayer, whose worship is expressed not in Sunday services and prayer gatherings only but also in their homes, their weekday work and the common things of life. I have a dream of a worshipping church.

I have a dream of a church which is a caring church—whose congregation is drawn from many races, nations, ages, and social backgrounds, and exhibits the unity and diversity of the family of God, whose fellowship is warm and welcoming, and never marred by anger, selfish-ness, jealousy or pride, whose members love one another with a pure heart fervently, forbearing one another, forgiving one another, and bearing one another's burdens, which offers friendship to the lonely, support to the weak, and acceptance to those who are despised and rejected by society, whose love spills over to the world outside, attractive, infectious, irresistible, the love of God himself. I have a dream of a caring church.

I have a dream of a church which is a serving church—which has seen Christ as the Servant and has heard his call to be a servant too, which is delivered from self-interest, turned inside out, and giving itself selflessly to the service of others, whose members obey Christ's command to live in the world, to permeate secular society, to be the salt of the earth and the light of the world, whose people share the good news of Jesus simply, naturally and enthusiastically with their friends, which diligently serves its own communities, residents and workers, families and single people, nationals and immigrants, old folk and little children, which is alert to the changing needs of society, sensitive and flexible enough to keep adapting its programme to serve more usefully, which has a global vision and is constantly challenging its young people to give their lives in service, and constantly sending its people out to serve. I have a dream of a serving church.

I have a dream of a church which is an expectant church—whose members can never settle down in material affluence or comfort, because they remember that they are strangers and pilgrims on earth, which is all the more faithful and active because it is waiting and looking for its Lord to return, which keeps the flame of the Christian hope burning brightly in a dark, despairing world, which on the day of Christ will not shrink from him in shame, but rise up joyfully to meet him. I have a dream of an expectant church.

Such is my dream of a living church. May all of us share this dream, and under God may the dream come true! [3]

That vision has clarified and underpinned the ministry at All Souls for the last 35 years, as well as inspiring many other churches around the world with a similar vision. I remember hearing it soon after it was given, and it has always shaped my vision of Church.

VISION IN THE BIBLE

The Bible is full of visions to inspire and encourage God's people. The book of Isaiah is a good Old Testament example. In Isaiah 2:1–4, the prophet gives the Jewish exiles a vision of a restored Jerusalem and a restored temple, with people of all nations streaming to it to hear the word of the Lord. In 11:1–10 we find a vision of a renewed and peaceful creation ('the wolf will live with the lamb', v. 6) flowing from the reign of a messianic king ('a shoot... from the stump of Jesse', v. 1), while in 40:1–31 there is a vision of the majesty and greatness of God that dwarfs all the world's ideas of greatness. In chapter 53 there is the famous vision of a suffering servant whose vicarious suffering brings forgiveness and salvation to God's people, while in Isaiah 61:1–2 we find a vision of a messianic Saviour whose anointed ministry will bring God's blessing to the poor, the brokenhearted, the captives and the prisoners. So many of Isaiah's prophecies aimed to inspire the Israelites with a fresh vision of the Lord God and his sovereign purposes, so that they would keep trusting him as they experienced the harsh realities of exile in Babylon.

Isaiah's messianic vision shaped Jesus' life and ministry. He reads the text of Isaiah 61:1–2 in the synagogue in Nazareth, right at the start of his public ministry, and says to the congregation, 'Today this scripture is fulfilled in your hearing.'[4] Similarly, Isaiah 53 shaped Jesus' understanding of his call and destiny, as we see from Mark 10:45 or Luke 22:37, where we find Jesus identifying with the suffering servant.

The first Christians were clearly shaped by Jesus' 'vision statements' in the Sermon on the Mount,[5] and by his commission to his followers in Matthew 28:16–20 and Acts 1:8. In Acts 2:42–47, Luke gives us a vision of the calling and priorities of a local church: teaching, worship, fellowship, prayer, sacraments, pastoral care, evangelism, signs, generous giving and hospitality. In other words, this is what happens in a community when people respond to Christ and are filled with the Spirit. This is life under the rule of

Jesus, a foretaste of the coming kingdom of God, when God will create a new heaven and a new earth. A vision statement is simply an articulation of these priorities.

Paul's epistles often give us a vision of the plan of salvation[6] before he spells out the implications for how we should live our lives.[7] Note the transition verse in Ephesians 4:1: 'I urge you to live a life worthy of the calling you have received.' He also shares with us God's vision for and calling on his life, often in reply to the critics of his ministry,[8] and these passages have become inspirational models for those involved in full-time Christian ministry.

John the apostle shares a vision of Jesus in Revelation 1:9–20, and the churches of Asia Minor are encouraged and challenged by prophetic visions in chapters 2 and 3. The apocalyptic visions that form the rest of the book (chapters 4—21) begin with a door opening into heaven, the voice of the Spirit calling John to enter to witness the eternal realities and the vision of God ruling on the throne of heaven.[9]

THE VALUE OF VISION

There are a number of reasons for church leaders to have a clearly articulated vision. Firstly, it will help us to know what God wants us to do. In one sense that should be obvious, because there are 'given' tasks and callings for the local church (worship, discipleship and mission), which we discover by a careful reading of the New Testament, and there are 'given' responsibilities for the church leader: preach and teach the Bible, mobilise the church into ministry and mission, pastor and nurture the flock, lead them in worship and prayer, and so on. So, you might ask, isn't it obvious what God wants us to 'do'? In this sense, yes, but every church is unique in its history, its membership and its setting, not to mention the fact that every church will be at a different spiritual stage. A vision statement, therefore, embraces the 'givens' of what a local church is called to be and to do, but is also sensitive to its unique context and history and spiritual temperature. This is the important listening process: the seven churches in Revelation were called to 'hear what the Spirit says to the churches',[10] and what the Spirit was saying to the church in Laodicea was not exactly the same as he was saying to the church at Ephesus. I suspect that the leaders of those seven churches, having heard God's particular word of encouragement and challenge to them, went away and asked, 'What shall we do about it? How should we shape church life differently in the light of what the Spirit has shown us?' At least, I hope they did that! So while developing a vision is, to some extent, about articulating the obvious, it is also about tailoring it into the unique local context. We therefore need the Word and the Spirit to help us: the Word to define and clarify, and the Spirit to give prophetic insight into our situation.

Secondly, a vision gives a great sense of purpose. The writer of Proverbs was absolutely right when he said, 'Where there is no vision, the people perish.'[11] Some churches are dying on their feet because they have lost that sense of what they are about. On the other hand, other churches are growing steadily because they have rediscovered God's vision for them as a local congregation, and this becomes a powerful internal dynamic that moves them forward.

Rick Warren, the senior pastor of Saddleback Community Church and author of *The Purpose Driven Church*, writes, 'If you want to build a healthy, strong and growing church you must spend time laying a solid foundation. This is done by clarifying in the minds of everyone involved exactly why the church exists and what it is supposed to do. There is an incredible power in having a clearly defined purpose statement.'[12]

Bill Hybels, Senior Pastor of Willow Creek Community Church in the States, goes even further:

Vision is at the very core of leadership. Take vision away from a leader and you cut out his or her heart. Vision is the fuel that leaders run on. It's the energy that creates action. It's the fire that ignites the passion of followers. It's the clear call that sustains focused effort year after year, decade after decade, as people offer consistent and sacrificial service to God.[13]

A little later he shares the depth of his own feelings about the vision that has motivated him to devote his life to serve at Willow Creek: 'I don't know how to explain the depth of feeling stirred in me by the ongoing wonder of Acts 2 churches. I can't count how many times I've fallen on my knees and said to God, "Nothing else does this to me. Clearly I was born for this."'[14]

Vision also provides us with a sound basis for unity. Every member of the church has their own agenda. So many church leaders are driven by the people who shout loudest ('Please can we have more worship', 'We must get out on the streets', 'We must be praying at 6am every morning', 'We must have 1662'). Some leaders fall over themselves to try to accommodate everyone's views. A much better way of doing Christian leadership is to focus on God's agenda for a local church, and to allow the New Testament to shape our vision of what God wants us to do. Then we can all unite around that shared purpose, which, all being well, will embrace many of the people's personal agendas too.

James Lawrence, creator of the Arrow Leadership course and author of *Growing Leaders*, says, 'Vision creates a sense of togetherness and accomplishment. People like to belong. One of the uses of the word fellowship in the New Testament is to "partner with a purpose". A clear vision helps people to know where they are going and work out the part they might play. The sense of "being in it together" is very important.'[15]

We should also note that vision allows us to concentrate our energies. Once we have identified our primary purposes, then we can shape church life around them. All our energies and all our activities are geared towards serving those great purposes. This will save us from becoming distracted by good and worthwhile things, but things that don't serve the main purposes of the church. A clear vision enables us to 'major on the majors'.[16] It is when light is focused through a magnifying glass that it can set a leaf on fire and even a bonfire ablaze; so when our efforts are focused on fulfilling God's vision for a local church, then we start having a significant impact on our society.

Finally, vision helps us to evaluate our progress. An archer who shoots arrows aimlessly into the sky will never know if he is improving; but when a target is put in front of him, he can immediately measure his progress. If his arrows fall 20 metres short of the target, that's fine, provided they're a bit closer than the previous week. Next week they may be ten metres short, and the week after that he starts to hit the target, and there's a wonderful sense of achievement. The day he hits the bulls eye, he's over the moon! A vision statement serves a similar kind of purpose as a target: it is there as a standard by which we can measure the health and effectiveness of our church. If we aim at nothing, we will certainly hit nothing, but if we know what we're going for, we can evaluate how we're doing. If we miss the mark a bit, that is OK, provided we made some progress from last year. Our joy when we start to hit the target will be very special!

WORD AND SPIRIT IN DEVELOPING A VISION

The first stage in developing a vision is a listening and discerning process, and it must start in prayer for wisdom and insight. This is not just a clinical, academic exercise of working out the key tasks of a local church; it is a careful, prayerful listening process as we discern God's purposes and plans for us and our people. God will have a unique bit of kingdom-building to do in our parish, and we will need wisdom and insight from heaven. Developing vision starts with us on our knees.

The next stage involves studying the Bible with our leaders, perhaps our staff team, key lay leaders and the church council. God's Word must shape and inspire any vision that is developed in the name of Christ. If the vision is not rooted in and bedded into the biblical revelation, then it won't be a revelation from God. It is

God's Word that is 'a lamp to my feet and a light for my path'.[17]

After I had spent three months as vicar at St John's in West Ealing, we planned a day away for the staff and the church council. We spent the morning studying the Bible and focusing on Matthew 5:1–12, Matthew 28:19–20, and especially Acts 2:42–47, with their emphasis on priorities for a Christian community. I asked, 'What is the calling of a local church?' and we wrote up on a flip chart what we discovered. In the afternoon we asked a slightly different question: 'If you could dream a dream for St John's, what would it look like?' Not surprisingly, the group came up with an identical list to the one we had produced in the morning. The Bible had shaped the vision.

The third stage is listening carefully to what the Spirit is saying in our unique context. Every church context is different, and this is where we have to know our patch and our people well. The same Spirit who has spoken to us through the biblical texts will now want to shape the vision into our particular situation. For example, an inner-city church in a multicultural parish may feel called to emphasise the importance of proclaiming the uniqueness of Christ among other faith communities in a loving and sensitive way, and serving the needs of the poor and the homeless as we share Christ with them. A city-centre church with a university on its doorstep, on the other hand, may feel a strong sense of responsibility to reach out to students and the academic staff. A rural group of parishes might see their primary sphere of witness as being an incarnational involvement in the life of their communities.

This sensitivity to context will also involve building on what is already there. Most parishes will have a long spiritual history, and it is fair to assume that the Holy Spirit has been at work long before we arrived. So it would be very disrespectful to the church members, not to mention grieving to the Holy Spirit, if, in our enthusiasm to develop a vision statement, we gave the impression that nothing had been happening before, but it was going to start right now! The way to avoid this is, partly, by asking people about their experiences and memories of being involved in the church over the years, and partly by looking carefully at some of the documentation that has been left as part of the church's spiritual heritage. Previous Annual Meeting reports, previous vision statements, the parish profile and so on will cast light on the spiritual history of the church, and will enable you to affirm the good bits that need to be built on and developed. By way of example, I knew when I arrived at St John's in 1999 that we needed to do some major reordering of the church crypt; the whole place looked tired and worn. I found a booklet in the archives that explained why a previous reordering had taken place in the 1970s. In it was a vision of St John's being a church for the community. That was a key part of what we were sensing the Spirit saying to us now: we too wanted to serve our community. So it was good to be able to say, 'St John's has always had a tradition of service in the community and that is why the crypt was reordered in the 1970s. It has served us well; and that's why we need to do it again for a new generation.' Longer-term members remembered that, and got on board for the new task.

The final stage in developing a vision is to draft a statement that articulates what you believe the Lord has been saying. This could be done on your own, but I did it with five key staff and lay leaders. We were very thrilled to come up with a concise, trinitarian statement about what we believed our calling to be at St John's. We took it back to the church council and they liked it, but helped us with some important refinements. We also asked a wise and trusted consultant to listen in on our discussions, and her wisdom, affirmation and insight were invaluable, too. We then presented the revised version to the annual church meeting and encouraged comment and feedback. I cannot emphasise enough how important this consultation process was in terms of ownership and support. If we had foisted on the church a vision statement which had been written behind the closed doors of the vicar's study, I doubt if anything would have been achieved. Shared ownership and common purpose are crucial. As Zachary Vernon has said, writing out of 25 years' ministry experience in Sydney, 'The power of a

common vision is a wonderful tool in modern Christian ministry...
vastly superior to a vision that is totally the senior minister's plan
which is imposed upon a church from on high.'[18]

WORD AND SPIRIT IN IMPLEMENTING A VISION

Developing a vision is the crucial beginning, but it will mean
nothing if it is not worked through into church life and allowed
to shape all that we do. Rick Warren talks about this as the most
difficult part of becoming a purpose-driven church: in his chapter
on 'Applying your purposes', he spells out the need to apply those
purposes rigorously to every part of the church. 'Assimilate new
members on purpose, programme around your purposes, educate
your people on purpose, start small groups on purpose, add staff
on purpose, structure on purpose, preach on purpose, budget on
purpose, calendar on purpose, and evaluate on purpose.'[19]

All this takes focused attention and an unwavering commitment. Here are what I have found to be five essential aspects of
implementing a vision from my experience. Firstly, preach on it
regularly, showing the biblical basis for it. We did so over a period
of three months and, at the end of this time, the staff said to me,
'Will, we don't think the church has really got it yet.' So we then
did it over again during the course of the following year. At the end
of that year, people were envisioned and excited. The Bible had
done its work.

Secondly, we worked out a five-year strategic plan to deliver the
vision. This involved dividing the whole of church life into about
15 areas, and then asking, 'How can we deliver the vision in each
particular area?' It meant having a longer-term aim of where we
wanted to be in five years' time, and having a realistic one-year
target about what could be achieved in the next twelve months.
This required openness to the Holy Spirit and sensitivity to his
promptings.

Thirdly, we kept bringing our staff and church council back to the vision, making sure that they had it firmly in their sights and were actively seeking to deliver it. For example, during the weekly staff meeting, each staff member took it in turns to talk about their areas in relation to the vision. What was going well, and what needed more effort and prayer? Likewise, we planned one church council a year to remind ourselves of the vision and to look closely at the five-year plan. I knew that if I didn't keep the leaders focused on delivering the vision, it would soon begin to slip off the radar.

Fourthly, I wrote my Vicar's Annual Report around it each year. The report would begin, 'As you are aware, we have an important vision that drives our church and motivates everything we do. Once again I would like to assess the past year in the light of this vision and see where things have been achieved and what still needs to be done.' I then looked at the year under the three headings of the vision statement: 'Glorifying the Father' (in other words, our worship), 'Growing as disciples of Jesus' (our discipleship) and 'Going out in the power of the Spirit' (our mission). This had a number of positive spin-offs: it signalled the high importance of the vision to the congregation, it gave us a way of evaluating how we were doing and what still needed to be done, and, most importantly, it caused us to give thanks to God for what he had done.

Finally, we included the vision on all our publicity: on the church website, on the termly programme card, on the noticeboards, in the welcome pack for newcomers, and in the information about small groups. This meant that no one could be in any doubt about what we believed God had called us to do by his Word and his Spirit.

CONCLUSION

In 1999, when I started out as vicar of St John's, I read these words of Rick Warren in his powerful book, *The Purpose Driven Church*: 'Many churches are barely surviving because they have no vision... Nothing discourages a church more than not knowing why it exists. On the other hand, the quickest way to reinvigorate a plateaued or declining church is to reclaim God's purpose for it and help the members understand the great tasks the church has been given by Christ.'[20] Nothing was more relevant to our situation: these words took on an almost prophetic significance for us. Thanks to God's Word and his Spirit, we developed a vision that gave us renewed purpose and direction, and, through it, the Lord continued to build his church. God's Word reminded us of the great purposes that God had called us into, and God's Spirit gave us fresh wisdom and prophetic insight into our immediate priorities. How we needed both!

Notes

1   Full text and video and audio of Martin Luther King's speech 'I have a dream': www.americanrhetoric.com/speeches/mlkihaveadream.htm
2   Bill Hybels, *Courageous Leadership* (Zondervan, 2002), p. 30
3   John Stott, *The Living Church* (IVP, 2007), pp. 179–182
4   Luke 4:16–21
5   Matthew 5:1–16
6   See, for example, Ephesians 1—3
7   See Ephesians 4—6
8   2 Corinthians 4:1–6; Colossians 1:28–29; Acts 20:17–24
9   Revelation 4:1
10 Revelation 2:7
11 Proverbs 29:18 (KJV)
12 Rick Warren, *The Purpose Driven Church* (Zondervan, 1995), p. 86
13 Hybels, *Courageous Leadership*, p. 31
14 Hybels, *Courageous Leadership*, p. 35
15 James Lawrence, *Growing Leaders* (BRF, 2004), p. 197
16 As the old saying goes, 'The main thing is to keep the main thing the main thing!'
17 Psalm 119:105
18 Zachary Veron, *Leadership on the Front Foot* (Anglican Press Australia, 2009), p. 165
19 Warren, *Purpose Driven Church*, p. 137–152
20 Warren, *Purpose Driven Church*, p. 87

WORKING IN TEAMS AND
MENTORING LEADERS

One of the greatest privileges of being in Christian ministry over the years has been working alongside a diverse range of gifted colleagues. I am so grateful that, when I was in parish ministry, God brought committed Christian workers alongside me whose gifts and experience not only complemented mine but also helped to cover my own limitations and shortcomings. From youth workers to administrators, from community workers to discipleship coordinators, from curates to outreach workers, it was always a team effort. Some were full-time, some part-time, and some volunteers or interns. Some came to us from other parts of the UK or the world; some emerged from within the church family as God's choice. But they were nearly always a blessing to me and to the churches we were serving. I couldn't have exercised effective leadership without them, and I echo the sentiment of Bill Hybels: 'I have learnt over the years that I am not strong enough to face the rigour of church work alone.'[1]

SHARED LEADERSHIP IN THE BIBLE

There are strong biblical foundations for doing ministry in teams. In Exodus 18:13–27, Moses gets some very wise advice from his father-in-law, Jethro, about how to cope with the pastoral and judicial load that is falling on his shoulders as the leader of the people of Israel. Jethro suggests that he choose trusted and godly people to help him. Moses follows this advice and appoints judges, who prove to be a blessing both to Moses and the people (vv. 22–23). It is worth considering what might have happened if God had not prompted Jethro to make this suggestion.

In the New Testament, Jesus chooses to share his ministry with twelve apostles. They are called to watch him, learn from him and then go out and do kingdom ministry themselves.[2] In Luke 10: 1–2, Jesus sends out 72 on mission, although, actually, only 36 units go out because they have to go in pairs. I think we can learn from this that we are not meant to do kingdom ministry on our own. We will need at least one companion to support us, pray for us and share the responsibility with us, says Jesus.

All leadership in the early Church appears to have been plural. In Acts 6:1–6, the apostles maintain their priorities of preaching and prayer by sharing administrative and pastoral responsibilities with seven other godly people. In Acts 13:1–3, Luke allows us to eavesdrop on the leaders' prayer meeting at Antioch, and we find a shared leadership of apostles, pastors, teachers, prophets and evangelists (they are all there, even though Luke only mentions two categories—prophets and teachers). It is the practical outworking of Ephesians 4:11–12: '[Christ] gave some to be apostles, some to be prophets, some to be evangelists, and some to be pastors and teachers, to prepare God's people for works of service.' Local church leadership is teamwork.

The Pastoral Epistles (1 and 2 Timothy and Titus) also talk of local church leadership in plural terms. In 1 Timothy 3, Paul gives Timothy some guidelines on the kind of qualities needed in the leaders of a local church. Although the overseer/bishop is spoken of in the singular (v. 1), suggesting that there is one senior pastor for a local congregation, Paul talks about the pastor sharing his ministry with deacons (plural, v. 8), who will carry out many of the administrative and pastoral tasks. This places the pastor's leadership firmly within the setting of a team.

In fact, we need to go further and say that all leadership in the New Testament is also seen as part of the church community that it serves, not as distinct from it. So Gordon Fee comments,

'Leadership in the New Testament people of God is never seen as outside or above the people themselves, but simply as part of the whole, essential to its well-being, but governed by the same set of "rules". They are not "set apart" by "ordination"; rather their gifts are part of the Spirit's work *among* the whole people.'[3] Likewise, James Lawrence, reflecting on the first six chapters of Acts, concludes, 'Those in leadership are part of the community, benefiting from its provision, care, and prayer as they serve as leaders.'[4] This in turn takes us back to the example of Jesus at the last supper, where he expresses his leadership of the apostolic community of disciples in terms of humble service and sacrifice. Jesus defines the task of Christian leadership as sacrificial service of the community to which we also belong: 'I have set you an example that you should do as I have done for you.'[5]

WORD AND SPIRIT IN APPOINTING STAFF

We have seen that the Word of God provides the warrant for appointing church staff and working in teams. We also know that the New Testament (especially the Pastoral Epistles) sets out the necessary criteria for Christian leadership, both in terms of giftings[6] and character.[7] On the basis of this biblical foundation we can approach our church council and talk to it about the need for shared leadership and the strategic need for certain staff to be appointed. However, we will need to be even more precise about why a particular staff member is needed if the council is going to give its backing and support the necessary appeal for a rise in the church's income. This is where we need to link back to the church's vision and argue the case from what we believe the Spirit has been saying to us about our ministry and mission in our unique context.

Three examples from my own experience can serve to illustrate how this might happen. Firstly, in Bristol, we had a strong sense of the Spirit calling us to share the gospel with the Asian community in the parish. The calling was incorporated into a vision statement that expressed our desire to see our church reflecting the social and racial mix of the parish. In order for this to happen, we made a case for appointing an experienced Asian outreach worker to come and spearhead the work, which led to two consecutive staff appointments—one being an outreach worker trained at All Nations College, and the other a Christian Pakistani evangelist who came to us under the auspices of the Church Mission Society. Secondly, in Ealing, we had a vision statement that spoke about us being called to 'grow as disciples of Jesus'. This led to us appointing a discipleship coordinator, covering areas such as small groups, prayer, training, discipleship courses and pastoral care. I had a 'picture' given to me during the appointment process that the coordinator would be somebody who would 'strengthen the pillars of the church', and that is precisely what the person appointed did in spiritual terms. Thirdly, also in Ealing, we had a growing sense of the Spirit calling us to bring the gospel of hope to our homeless community, whom local churches had been feeding for many years through the Ealing Soup Kitchen. It resulted in eight churches partnering to appoint an outreach worker to deepen our ministry to the homeless and share the gospel with them, and this in turn led to a new congregation known as Café Church, which at the time of writing has about 60–70 members.

The key point here is that staff should be appointed in line with the vision of the church, which in turn needs to be in line with what the Word and the Spirit have been saying. Once the vision is clear, staff appointments can follow to implement and facilitate the vision. But, I hear someone saying, how can we pay for it, when the church is so strapped for cash? Again, both Word and Spirit are needed to provide the resources for God's work: the Word teaches us about Christian stewardship and generosity, and the Spirit opens our hearts to give generously and sacrificially in response to the Word. But what if the church is already giving all it can? Well, there are still a number of different options: there may be a salary freed up if an existing staff member moves on. Or, if we are in an inner-city or small rural parish, we will be able to obtain funding from a grant-making trust or a Christian organisation, especially if the new post is community-focused. In Bristol, we managed to secure £250,000 from the Single Regeneration Budget in order to develop our Family Centre Project, which meant that we could reach out to local families through a whole raft of activities and groups, with paid staff to run them. The great missionary to China, Hudson Taylor, once said, 'God's work, done in God's way, will never lack God's supply.'

The interview process will also need God's Word and God's Spirit to guide us to the right person. Obviously we need to use our God-given common sense and intuitive wisdom, but we are also looking to God to show us the person of his choice. Remember that Jesus spent the whole night in prayer before he chose his twelve disciples,[8] so we certainly need the prompting and guidance of the Holy Spirit in all our decision-making. Sometimes I have been genuinely surprised by the person who emerges as the strongest candidate; sometimes it has been blindingly obvious from the moment they applied. But the Bible too will shape the decision on who to appoint: do they have a growing relationship with Jesus, do they long to share the gospel with others, do they fashion their life according to the Scriptures, and are they showing the fruit of the Spirit? We cannot afford to bypass issues of character and lifestyle in preference for gifting and experience.

WORD AND SPIRIT IN SUPPORTING STAFF

Appointing the right staff is the beginning of an exciting adventure, but they will need supervision, support and encouragement. There are lots of practical ways to do this: setting some realistic targets for the first six months, getting to know them (and their family, if appropriate) socially and informally, having regular support sessions with them, watching them in action, and giving them some positive and honest feedback. They will value our steering and wisdom, but they will also need plenty of space to do their own thing and exercise their ministry in the way that God has shaped and equipped them.

Most importantly, we can read the Bible with them and pray together, although this is usually done at staff prayers or staff meetings. During the course of a week, at the churches where I ministered, we would do this in a whole variety of ways: by working through a book of the Bible, by praying for each other and our respective areas of ministry, by giving time to worship, praise and thanksgiving, by interceding for the church and for the world, by prayer-walking around the parish or by using Anglican or Celtic forms of Morning Prayer. What was important was that these staff devotionals were times of real engagement with God, through feeding on his Word and being filled with his Spirit. The exacting demands of Christian ministry required nothing less.

WORD AND SPIRIT IN IDENTIFYING FUTURE LEADERS

When God calls us into a position of ministry and influence for his kingdom, we will inevitably leave a legacy. But the legacy we leave should not be about how amazing we were, and how we managed to achieve so much; the best legacy we can leave in a church is one that ensures that God's work continues to grow and expand after we have gone. That can happen only if we have invested in a new generation of leaders who will carry on where we leave off. Even better, they will already be doing ministry by the time we leave, so that God's work continues seamlessly without us.

This is nothing new about this. If we read the story of the Exodus,[9] we see that Moses was one of the leaders in the Old Testament who had such a huge influence on the people of Israel that it would be very difficult for anyone to follow him. Who could possibly fill his shoes and give leadership to God's people for the next stage of Israel's journey? The answer was two people: Joshua and Caleb. They were God's people for that next stage, and they led the Israelites out of the wilderness and into the promised land. Did they suddenly appear at the right moment? No; Moses had invested in them with his time, his heart, his wisdom and his passion for God's glory.

The same could be said of Elijah. He was a giant in his day, in terms of the significance of his ministry: the contest on Mount Carmel put God right back in the centre of Israel's life.[10] Who could follow him? The answer is that Elisha could. Why? Because Elijah had invited Elisha to be with him and watch him do his ministry.[11] It is not until 2 Kings 2 that Elijah's mantle actually falls to Elisha, when Elijah is taken to be with the Lord, but by then he has learnt about the challenges and demands of prophetic ministry.

The same could be said of Jesus, too: although he had a place in his heart for everybody, he invested a disproportionate amount of time in teaching and training his twelve disciples, letting them watch him do the ministry of the kingdom of God, sending them out on mission themselves and debriefing with them afterwards. Right up to the end (even at the last supper) he was talking them through what it means to be servant leaders, and modelling it for them by washing their feet. He clearly invested in a few for the sake of the many.

Paul was a missionary, evangelist, pastor, teacher and theologian, all rolled into one. Who could follow him? The answer is: the people he invested in, such as Timothy, who travelled with him on his missionary journeys, watched him minister and then took over the leadership of the church at Ephesus. There is no doubt that there is a good biblical precedent for nurturing future leaders.

Who should we invest in if we are leaders of a local church? We must allow the Holy Spirit to guide us. Obviously our staff team, if we have one, will need (and expect) our interest in and nurturing of them and their ministries. We should also invest in the leaders of our midweek and Sunday ministries, such as home groups, youth and children's groups, prayer ministry, community outreach groups, preachers and worship leaders. We can take an interest in their ministries, see what morale is like, and notice if anyone is struggling.

Ministries thrive under the interest and encouragement of the church leader.

We should also be sure to invest time in those who are sensing God's call into full-time Christian ministry. We started a group at my church in Ealing called the TOM group (Thinking of Ministry), and invited along anyone who wanted to explore the possibility, making it clear that there was no obligation to keep coming if their questions had been resolved and they wanted to leave. To my surprise, we had about ten people over a three- to four-year period. They were at different stages of vocation, some going on to be ordained, some going into local church ministries like youth work, some going into cross-cultural mission work, and others deciding that God was calling them to stay where they were. Sometimes we had guest speakers at the group; sometimes we had discussions on the challenges of full-time ministry; sometimes we studied the biblical call narratives such as Isaiah 6 or Jeremiah 1. As the group continued, it was exciting to see God calling people into leadership, ministry and mission.

WORD AND SPIRIT IN MENTORING FUTURE LEADERS

We can sometimes choose to invest time in particular individuals, as the Holy Spirit prompts us. I developed a sense of call to Christian leadership through the personal nurturing of a Ridley Hall ordinand while I was at Cambridge as an undergraduate. In my turn, when I was at Ridley, I read the Bible and prayed with a number of undergraduates during my three years of training, some of whom went on into full-time Christian ministry, and I guess they did the same thing with others. It reminds me of Paul's words to Timothy: 'The things you have heard me say in the presence of many witnesses, entrust to reliable people who will also be qualified to teach others.'[12] In parish ministry, too, there have always been certain people that I wanted to nurture individually, often on instinct, sometimes because I have sensed their potential for leadership and always (I hope) in obedience to the Holy Spirit.

As I mentored them, I aimed to invest in them a number of things. Firstly, I wanted them to know my convictions from the Bible, those foundational beliefs that have shaped my life and given it meaning and purpose: the inspiration and authority of Scripture, the grace and goodness of God, the death and resurrection of Jesus, the power and gifts of the Holy Spirit, the challenges and opportunities of mission, the return of Christ and the certainty of judgment, and the prospect of a new heaven and a new earth. Secondly, I shared something of my experience of God's grace and power, to show how belief works out in practice, how I have sensed God's presence at various times, how I have handled difficult situations, how God has helped me when I needed him, and how I have had the courage to share Jesus with neighbours and friends. I encouraged those whom I was mentoring to ask any questions they wanted, and tried to be transparent and honest and real in response. Thirdly, I shared my passion for God's work, telling them about my call to the ministry and what I did in a normal week. I shared some good experiences of seeing God at work in parish ministry, and let them laugh with me about the funny times. I tried to give them a feel of what it is like to be in Christian leadership and, if they asked about how they might explore a call to ministry, I took time to explain the process.

Finally, I gave them a vision of what God can do, helping them to see how awesome God is and that nothing is impossible for him. I took them to Ephesians 3:20: 'Now to him who is able to do immeasurably more than all we ask or imagine, according to his power that is at work within us...' I tried to get them excited about the power of the Holy Spirit in ministry and mission, and inspired them with a vision for change. I aimed to reassure them that God is not limited by the failings and shortcomings of his Church.

What are the foundational elements in this kind of mentoring process, whether for existing or future leaders? I would suggest the following:

- We can give others our time: amid all the demands of ministry, this has to be a priority. Put the leaders meetings in the diary a year in advance if necessary, and don't let anything budge them. At the end of a one-to-one session, book up the next session. We need to be ruthlessly disciplined in our diary planning because it is so important!
- We can give them our love: 1 Thessalonians 2:8 says, 'We loved you so much that we were delighted to share with you not only the gospel of God but our lives as well, because you had become so dear to us.' Paul went well beyond simply giving people time: he shared himself with them, attending to their every need.
- We can give them our wisdom. I don't mean that we know it all but that, because of our greater experience of ministry, we will have picked up some important lessons and principles about the kingdom of God and about being a Christian leader. We can share that wisdom and give them a glimpse of how ministry works.
- We can give them our modelling. We can let them see us doing ministry, not just on Sundays but during the week as well (if they are free). We can take them on a funeral or baptism visit, take them to see someone in hospital, let them watch us pray for the sick or pray for someone to be released from demonic oppression, let them see us take a school assembly, invite them to help us lead a Christian Basics course, or take them on a mission trip to Africa (we took three teams out to Uganda).
- We can give them our permission. All being well, having watched us, they will want to have a go, but they need us to turn to them and say, 'It's your turn now.' We don't just leave them to it, but watch them carefully so that we can give them some constructive feedback. If they are going to preach regularly or become a pastoral visitor, they may need some kind of official licence from the church authorities.
- We can give them our encouragement. Of course, there will be areas for improvement, and we can sensitively work on those, but what they will need most is our overriding encouragement.

'That was amazing for a first time! That was fabulous! Well done.' It will give them the confidence to have another go.

- We can give them our prayers. When Paul wrote to churches or to individuals, he went out of his way to assure them of his prayers: 'always giving thanks' and 'constantly remembering you in my prayers'.[13] What a blessing that would have been to them, not just because they would have been encouraged that the apostle was praying for them but because God moves in answer to prayer. It is through prayer that God accomplishes his purposes in us, so we gladly bring those we are mentoring to God in prayer: 'Lord, please continue the good work you have begun.'[14]

CONCLUSION

We saw earlier that John Stott and David Watson were two evangelical leaders who exercised a huge influence for Christ during the second half of the 20th century (and beyond), but who mentored them into Christian leadership?

In John Stott's case, it was an Anglican vicar called Eric Nash, or 'Bash' as he was affectionately known. He founded the Scripture Union camps at Iwerne Minster,[15] and Stott pays an enormous tribute to him in one of his books:

I thank God for the man who led me to Christ and for the extraordinary devotion with which he nurtured me in the early years of my Christian life. He wrote to me every week for, I think, seven years. He also prayed for me every day... I can only begin to guess what I owe, under God, to such a faithful friend and pastor.[16]

David Watson's early mentor was David Sheppard, the England cricket captain who went on to be Bishop of Liverpool:

David Sheppard invited me round to his rooms at Ridley Hall... Almost every week throughout the academic year I went round to talk to David, often for as much as three hours at a time, and he began to lay a foundation for my faith... the foundation of Jesus Christ. Normally we read a passage from the Bible together, David choosing a passage carefully each week to meet my particular need at that stage... It is impossible to stress how vital these sessions were for me. Without them, humanly speaking, I should never have survived as a Christian.[17]

These two examples show the influence that careful and prayerful mentoring can have. The Word of God plays a vital role as emerging leaders are grounded and envisioned by the central truths of the Bible. The Spirit of God also plays his part, identifying, calling, empowering and equipping them. That is how future leaders are identified and nurtured and how we ensure that the legacy we leave is that God's work goes on from strength to strength.

Notes

1   Bill Hybels, *Courageous Leadership* (Zondervan, 2002), p. 248
2   Luke 6:12–16; 9:1–6
3   Gordon Fee, *Listening to the Spirit in the Text* (Eerdmans, 2000), p. 124
4   James Lawrence, *Growing Leaders* (BRF, 2004), p. 235
5   John 13:15
6   1 Timothy 4:14; 2 Timothy 1:6
7   1 Timothy 3:1–10; 2 Timothy 2:22–26
8   Luke 6:12
9   Exodus 5—15
10   1 Kings 18:16–40
11   1 Kings 19—21
12   2 Timothy 2:2 (TNIV)
13   See Philippians 1:3–4
14   See Philippians 1:6
15   See John Eddison (ed.), *Bash: A Study in Spiritual Power* (Marshall, 1983)
16   John Stott, *Guard the Gospel* (IVP, 1973), p. 29
17   David Watson, *You Are My God* (Hodder, 1983), pp. 24–25

MOBILISING EVERY MEMBER INTO MINISTRY

Our contemporary culture is obsessed with the 'body beautiful', as evidenced by the fascination with celebrity culture, the ever-changing trends of fashion and the increasing demand for cosmetic surgery by those who can afford it. The positive side to all this is that we, as human beings, are meant to care for our bodies and look after our health through regular exercise, healthy eating and adequate sleep. It doesn't stop the inevitable onslaught of ageing or make us immune from sickness or disease, but it keeps us in shape and gives us a better chance of staying healthier for longer. To put it the other way round, neglecting our bodies (and our humanity) diminishes our effectiveness in living and functioning to the full.

Christian leaders should also have a passion for the 'body beautiful', but in a different sense. One of Paul's favourite images of the Church was the 'body of Christ'.[1] I don't think it is a coincidence that churches which are flourishing (whatever their size) are usually led by ministers who not only love their flock but are passionate about seeing the church become all that Christ intended. Rick Warren, overseeing an extraordinary growth of his church in the USA, expressed this passion sublimely: 'I love the church of Jesus Christ with all my heart. Despite all its faults (due to our sinfulness) it is still the most magnificent concept ever created. It has been God's chosen instrument of blessing for two thousand years... It is worth giving our lives for and it deserves our best.'[2] Similarly, Bill Hybels, heading up the Willow Creek Community Church in Illinois, waxes lyrical about the 'body beautiful':

There is nothing like the local church when it is working right. Its beauty is indescribable. Its power is breathtaking. Its potential is unlimited. It comforts the grieving and heals the broken in the context of community. It builds bridges to seekers and offers truth to the confused. It provides resources for those in need and opens its arms to the forgotten, the downtrodden and the disillusioned. It breaks the chains of addictions, frees the oppressed and offers belonging to the marginalised of this world. Whatever the capacity for human suffering, the church has a greater capacity for healing and wholeness... No other organisation on earth is like the church. Nothing even comes close.[3]

Likewise, John Stott, having served the church community at All Souls, Langham Place, for all of his ministerial life, wrote about his convictions concerning the Church in one of his last books, *The Living Church—Convictions of a Lifelong Pastor*. In it he wrote:

We are not only committed to Christ, we are also committed to the body of Christ... For the church lies at the very centre of the eternal purpose of God... the church is God's new community. For his purpose, conceived in a past eternity, being worked out in history, and to be perfected in a future eternity, is not just to save isolated individuals... but rather to build his church, that is, to call out of the world a people for his own glory... we long to see it continually reformed and renewed by the word and the Spirit of God.[4]

Similarly, Nicky Gumbel, Vicar of Holy Trinity Brompton (one of the largest Anglican congregations in the UK), has written:

The church is made up of the people belonging to God, who are bound together in love as a family with Christ in their midst. They represent Christ to the world, loving their Lord as a bride loves the bridegroom, and being loved by him... What a place to be—it should be near heaven on earth.[5]

THE PRIESTHOOD AND MINISTRY OF ALL BELIEVERS

If the church of the Reformation period (16th and 17th centuries) rediscovered 'the *priesthood* of all believers', so that every Christian could enjoy access to God through the saving work and priesthood of Christ, then it can be plausibly argued that the church of the periods of Revival and Renewal (18th, 19th and 20th centuries) rediscovered 'the *ministry* of all believers', so that every Christian has a calling and gifting to serve Christ in the Church and the world.[6] This is exactly what Paul was telling us when he employed the metaphor of 'the body of Christ' for the Church. This image is certainly about the vital union between Christ ('the head') and his people ('the body'),[7] and also emphasises the unity of the Church (one body with many parts; 'one body and one Spirit').[8] But the main point of the metaphor is that the Church is a functioning unit, a ministering community and a serving people with different giftings and ministries ('different kinds of gifts... different kinds of service... different kinds of working').[9] This is why Paul talks about spiritual gifts in three of the four main passages on the body of Christ.[10] We can't miss it: the Church is the body of Christ, equipped with the gifts of the Spirit, to build up Christ's body by acts of ministry and service, and so glorify Christ by becoming like him, 'attaining to the whole measure of the fullness of Christ'.[11] Every Christian has a gift, every believer has a ministry and so all followers of Jesus are 'charismatics' in the Pauline sense of Romans, Corinthians and Ephesians. The gifts of the Spirit belong inseparably and irrevocably to the biblical concept of the Church as the body of Christ.[12]

I have emphasised this point because it is well known that some parts of the Church have a 'cessationist' theology, arguing that the gifts of the Spirit died out with the end of the apostolic era and the closing of the canon of Scripture.[13] Their arguments, arising from a noble desire to uphold and defend the authority and sufficiency of the Scriptures, have been thoroughly examined and tested in a number of places and (in my view) found to be wanting.[14] What we need to note is that nowhere in the New Testament (especially not 1 Corinthians 13!) is it suggested that the spiritual gifts are for the apostolic era only. The Church in Acts had spiritual gifts in operation alongside the apostolic teaching without compromise, conflict or contradiction (except where some 'revelations' had to be challenged because of a departure from the apostolic gospel),[15] so why shouldn't we operate with both? While we all agree that we want to be faithful to the apostolic gospel and teachings, so we should also be faithful to the teaching of Paul on the use of spiritual gifts. Even when writing to the Corinthian church, which, while being full of charismatic gifts, was desperately immature, divided and sinful, Paul condemns not the spiritual gifts but rather the behaviour of the Corinthians. In fact, he explains the real purpose and appropriate use of the gifts of the Spirit, and then encourages them to be used more and more.

Further, if the spiritual gifts ceased at the end of the apostolic era, then so did the gifts of teaching, serving and administration that are included in Paul's lists. This surely can't be the case. If we argue that 'word gifts' continued while others didn't (a case often made from Ephesians 4:11), then think about the title 'evangelist'. Peter, Paul, Stephen and Philip were known as the evangelists in the early church and they all used spiritual gifts and experienced miracles in the course of their evangelistic ministry. Is it possible that Paul's definition of an evangelist in Ephesians 4 would have excluded this dimension?

We should remember, too, that the purpose of 'signs and wonders' was not simply to testify to the divinity of Jesus (even though some miracles were, of course, unique to him). Otherwise, why and how did the early Christians do very similar works? Nor were they used simply to validate apostolic authority, as Philip and Stephen did miraculous works but were not designated apostles,[16] and Paul indicates that miracles were happening in the churches of Galatia and Corinth too.[17] In fact, James expects healings to occur at the laying on of hands with prayer in all the churches to which he writes.[18] Instead, signs and wonders were tangible evidence of the presence of the kingdom of God, the future reign of God breaking in now because of Christ, until he returns to bring in the fullness of his kingdom.

The cessationists' claim that miracles in the Bible clustered in special periods of revelation, and that the last period was the apostolic era, is not supported by the biblical evidence, which shows miracles, prophecy and healings to be happening throughout the biblical narrative from Genesis onwards.[19] Such an argument also ignores the wealth of historical evidence of miraculous events throughout church history.[20] Even if 90 per cent of these claims were proved to be false, the ten per cent of credible claims would still be a denial of the cessationist position. The God of the Bible never changes; Jesus Christ is the same yesterday, today and for ever, and the power of the Holy Spirit is always immeasurably greater than we could imagine. Why would he suddenly stop behaving in the way that the Bible itself has helped us to understand and believe?

There is much more that could be said. However, the purpose of citing these arguments against the cessationist position is not to score theological points but to uphold the authority of the Scriptures by reinstating the teaching of Paul about the ministry of the body of Christ, and to uphold the sovereignty of the Spirit who gives good gifts to the body of Christ for ministry and service, distributing them 'as he determines' (1 Corinthians 12:11). What this means in practice is that those who love the 'word gifts' (teaching, pastoral care, evangelism) can't say to those who love the 'supernatural' or more miraculous gifts (miracles, prophecy, healing, tongues), 'I don't need you!', and vice versa (v. 21). All the gifts of the Spirit are about building up the body of Christ. All of them are intended to glorify Christ. All of them are, therefore, about the gospel and should never be seen as separate from the saving work of Christ on the cross. Gospel ministry involves spiritual gifts, and spiritual gifts are an integral part of gospel ministry. How did they ever get separated?[21]

Jim Packer, in his generous and honest assessment of the

Charismatic movement, talks about the emphasis on 'every-member ministry' as being one of its features which calls for 'unambiguous approval when biblically assessed'. Referring to Paul's vision in Ephesians 4, he says:

Charismatics take this vision seriously. They insist that active service on the part of each believer is the only regimen under which any church can mature; they deny that preaching alone can mature a church, if it is detached from meaningful mutual ministry; and they urge constantly that all Christians must find and use their powers of service to others… loving speech, loving action, loving care, loving prayer, as the case may be. [22]

Rick Warren talks about how every-member ministry is strongly emphasised at Saddleback:

We teach that every Christian is created for ministry (Ephesians 2:10), saved for ministry (2 Timothy 1:9), called into ministry (1 Peter 2:9–10), gifted for ministry (1 Peter 4:10), authorised for ministry (Matthew 28:18–20), commanded to minister (Matthew 20:26–28), to be prepared for ministry (Ephesians 4:11–12), needed for ministry (1 Corinthians 12:27), accountable for ministry and will be rewarded according to his or her ministry (Colossians 3:23–24). [23]

What, then, is the role of church leaders in all of this? Paul says in Ephesians 4:12 that the work of pastors and teachers is 'to equip the saints for the work of ministry' (RSV) or 'to prepare God's people for works of service' (NIV). So, when we talk about potential ordinands as 'going into the ministry', it is a complete and unbiblical misnomer. What we really want is *the church to go into ministry*, and our job as pastors and teachers is to help them to do that. That is where the ministries of the Word and the Spirit come into play.

ALLOWING THE WORD TO MOBILISE PEOPLE INTO MINISTRY

Pauls tells Timothy that the purpose of the 'inspired' Scriptures, in addition to making us 'wise for salvation', is 'so that all God's people may be thoroughly equipped for every good work'.[24] There are a number of ways the Bible does this, as it is preached and taught by church leaders and studied in small groups. Firstly, it shows us models and examples of Christian ministry to inspire us, such as Moses, Esther and Daniel in the Old Testament, and Mary, Paul and Barnabas in the New. Secondly, the Bible gives us a vision of the range and variety of gifts and ministries, from pastoral care to evangelism, from teaching to speaking prophetic words, from prayer for healing to administration, and from generous giving to leadership. It also defines what these ministries are and how they should be used, often by cross-reference to the early church in Acts. Thirdly, it defines the values that underpin all Christian ministries: a servant heart, a passion for Christ's glory, a sacrificial love, a holiness of life, an expectation that God will work, and a willingness to share the gospel. In all these ways, God speaks to his people and calls them into costly Christian service in the church, the workplace, the home, the community or the wider world.

One way we mobilised people into ministry in Ealing was to plan a five-week sermon series around Rick Warren's SHAPE course,[25] with a special midweek course running alongside it for people to join, to explore God's calling on their life into ministry. SHAPE is an acronym for Spiritual gifts, Heart, Abilities, Personality and Experience, helping people find their 'shape' for ministry. Under 'Spiritual gifts', we worked through the lists in 1 Corinthians 12 and Romans 12 and asked people to see what gifts God was giving to them. Under 'Heart' we asked what they felt passionate about, using passages like Acts 20:17–35 and Romans 10. Under 'Abilities' we asked them to think about their natural gifts and talents, looking at how God used Joseph's natural leadership and administrative ability in Egypt.[26] Under 'Personality', we got them to consider the way they were 'wired' (extravert or introvert, task-orientated or people-orientated, and so on) and looked at how God used someone like impetuous and outspoken Peter, with all his energy and enthusiasm, to become the leader of the early church.[27] Under 'Experience', we explored what people had done or been through, and how those experiences could equip them to serve others, because the Bible teaches us that no experience is wasted in God's kingdom purposes.[28]

Through this course, we gradually saw more and more people find the area of ministry that God was calling them into. Some people who had been sitting quietly in the background came forward and said that they felt God prompting them to get involved in one area of ministry or another. Others decided that God was moving them from one area of ministry into another, a decision based less on a sense of duty and more on a passion to make a difference. Others decided they needed to lay down a ministry after many years and take a sabbatical, so that they came back into ministry a year or two later with fresh energy and vision.

Another way we mobilised people in Ealing was to start a group for men who had been Christians for over 20 years. We did this because I (and one or two others) noticed that a lot of the mature Christian men in the church were not involved in frontline ministries; nor were they mentoring younger men into areas of ministry. They had been involved in the past (serving on the church council or helping with the youth work or prayer ministry team), but now they seemed to have become a bit weary and had lost some of their passion for God's work. My co-leader and I believed that we needed to allow the Bible to re-envision these men for Christian ministry, so we started to meet each month to study the Sermon on the Mount, using Dallas Willard's book, *The Divine Conspiracy*.[29] Gradually, over the weeks and months, fresh vision for the Lord's work came into their hearts and lives, and I noticed, a year on, that almost all of them were getting stuck into various key ministries again. I'm reminded of Martin Luther's words, spoken in a different context but equally true in this situation: 'I did nothing; the Word did it all.'[30]

ALLOWING THE SPIRIT TO MOBILISE PEOPLE INTO MINISTRY

As people study the Bible or listen to it being preached, the Spirit is already at work, calling and equipping them into ministry. He does this in a number of ways.

Firstly, the Spirit gives people a vision and a desire to serve. Acts 20:22–24 is an extraordinary passage because it gives us a window into the heart of the apostle Paul. What is his deepest desire and strongest passion in life? 'If only I may finish the race and complete the task the Lord Jesus has given me—the task of testifying to the gospel of God's grace' (v. 24). What is fuelling and driving this passion? 'And now, compelled by the Spirit, I am going to Jerusalem, not knowing what will happen to me there' (v. 22). This 'compelling' is more than just divine guidance through the Spirit's prompting; it is a compulsion that arises out of a deep devotion and gratitude to Christ for his sacrifice on the cross: 'For Christ's love compels us, because we are convinced that one died for all... that those who live should live no longer for themselves but for him.'[31] Hence Paul says in Acts 20, 'I consider my life as worth nothing to me' (v. 24). The Spirit fills his heart with love for Christ and compels him to go, whatever the cost.

Secondly, the Spirit brings gifts to the body of Christ for ministry and service. Although Paul says in Ephesians 4 that the gifts are given by the risen and ascended Christ (vv. 7–11), which clearly links the spiritual gifts with the gospel and is another reason for not seeing them as separate and dispensable, he states in 1 Corinthians 12 that spiritual gifts are a 'manifestation of the Spirit... for the common good' (v. 7); and again in verse 11: 'All these are the work of one and the same Spirit, and he gives them to each one, just as he determines.' In other words, although Christ authorises and sends the gifts, it is the Spirit who brings them to us and quickens them in us. So every Christian will have some gifting, whether they realise it or not ('To each one... is given', v. 7). Paul also encourages us to be open to receive new or different gifts,[32] although we should never expect to have all the gifts,[33] nor should we be envious or feel inferior because of the gifts of others.[34]

Thirdly, the Spirit works through the gifts that he brings. Through gifts of teaching he illuminates the eternal gospel truths of Scripture and applies them into the lives of God's people. Through gifts of prophecy he speaks a particular word of challenge or encouragement to a particular situation at a particular time to help us to be faithful to Christ. Through gifts of administration and leadership he brings order, direction and discipline into church life, helping us to function as the body of Christ. Through gifts of miracles he displays the power and glory of Christ. Through gifts of service he allows God's people to display the humility and grace of Christ. Through gifts of generosity he provides for the daily needs and future growth of the Church of Christ. Through gifts of evangelism he proclaims the truth of Christ and draws people to faith. Through gifts of tongues he allows us to pray to Christ with great intimacy in the language of angels. Through words of knowledge and wisdom he permits us to see and understand spiritual truths about Christ and his word that are hidden from human sight and natural understanding. Through gifts of healing he shows the compassion of Christ, reversing the effects of the fall and bearing witness to the new creation that awaits the Lord's return.[35] The key point to note again here is that the gifts of the Spirit are integral to gospel ministry, not something distinct or distracting from it or irrelevant to it. They are *all* about glorifying Jesus, for that is the Spirit's special work. If the early church received these gifts thankfully as vital bits of equipment for the ministry and mission that Jesus had given it to do, then shouldn't we receive them with the same humility, grace and gratitude?

Fourthly, the Spirit anoints and blesses the gifts that he gives. This is closely related, I believe, to the empowering by the Spirit for gospel ministry and the filling with the Spirit to help us to live a life worthy of the gospel,[36] for the gifts of the Spirit are integral to gospel ministry and Christian living. Timothy had a focus on gospel ministry when he took on the leadership of the church at Ephesus, and he was told by Paul to 'fan into flame the gift of God, which is in you through the laying on of my hands'.[37] If this refers to a spiritual gift (as many commentators think it does: leadership or teaching is commonly suggested), then 'fanning into flame' implies fresh anointing and empowering with the Spirit's fire. One of the reasons I have so valued attendance at Christian conferences such as New Wine is that it gives an opportunity to receive prayer for a fresh anointing of God's Spirit upon me. Many others, in the thick of Christian ministry, have said the same.

Finally, the Spirit entrusts gifts and ministries at the appropriate time. One of our tasks as church leaders is to try to find the right people for the right jobs when vacancies arise. In some ways, it is easier if people have been on something like the SHAPE course, heard God's call into a ministry and come to their church leader, saying, 'I would like to help to run a home group, or work with the youth ministry, or in the parish office, or on the pastoral team.' Obviously we still have to test their call and make sure that we think God is calling them. But at least the offer is there, and they can be deployed if appropriate. However, it is much harder for church leaders when a key vacancy arises (the youth leaders are moving suddenly to a new part of the country, for example) and there is no one obvious to fill the gap, often because suitable people are already overbusy elsewhere. This is when it is important to know that the Holy Spirit is working alongside us. He knows about the vacancy and he has been preparing someone for it. Our job is to pray and ask the Lord who that person might be. Although this is not a magic formula that always produces the right person (and, yes, we can make mistakes in our judgments about suitability or gifting), I have found that the Holy Spirit has often led me to people he has been preparing.

Let me give a few examples from my experience in Ealing.

Due to a change of circumstances, our churchwarden in Ealing generously offered to give a couple of days a week to help with some ministry in the church—whatever I felt was appropriate. I thanked him and said I would think and pray about it, and get back to him in due course. There were many areas where he could have helped, but I had an intuition that his passion was evangelism. At that time, our curate was heading up the Alpha courses as well as running the youth work, and he needed relieving of some of the pressure. I said to the churchwarden, 'Mark, how would you like to be our evangelism coordinator, organising and running Alpha courses, planning guest services and events, training the church in personal evangelism, and so on?' He replied, 'That's perfect! Just what I hoped you would ask me to do. If you had asked me to do administration or pastoral visiting, I would have had to say no!' The Holy Spirit had been saying the same thing to both of us, and many people came to Christ during his ministry over seven years.

Another example would be a role that developed from a complaint at the Annual Meeting. A young couple in the church bemoaned the fact that we were not encouraging more people to join home groups. They argued that these groups were very important for spiritual growth and discipleship, and were also places of pastoral care and support. Could we not give them a much higher profile and aim to get 70–80 per cent of the church into groups? It was music to my ears! More than that, I found myself listening to them and thinking, 'You would be perfect as our home group coordinators.' I approached them after the meeting and suggested it. They looked a bit shocked and made jokes about never complaining about anything again, but said 'Yes' a few days later. They were just right for the new role: passionate about Bible study, enthusiastic about fellowship and gifted administratively; most importantly, through them, numbers joining groups started to go up. It seemed that the Holy Spirit was preparing them for this role by giving them a holy discontent with the present situation, and then helping them to realise that they could do something about it.

Let me also tell you about a retired social worker who had run the bookstall faithfully for years. I felt that God had more in store for her, so, when the vacancy for churchwarden arose, I asked her to consider standing for election because of her Christian maturity and wisdom—and she got elected. In fact, I would say she had a gift of wisdom, often sharing thoughts in staff meetings or church council that gave us biblical clarity and direction to move us forward. She also had a prophetic gifting, which she used occasionally in a very modest and humble way. I remember her sharing a 'word' with me on the Sunday that we began a major rebuilding project in the crypt: 'I sensed the Lord saying to us during the worship, "As you start the building work downstairs, don't neglect the spiritual building work upstairs."' I took that very seriously as a reminder to keep focused on discipleship and evangelism, and we planned a special Lent course on spiritual disciplines that year as a consequence of the Spirit's prompting. Her most significant ministry, however, was in the area of pastoral care, heading up the pastoral team with extraordinary devotion and love, bringing comfort and grace into the lives of the elderly, the sick and those with special needs. God did indeed have more in store for her.

There were others too: the prayerful older woman who described a burning sensation in her hands whenever she prayed for the sick, whom we quickly drafted on to the prayer ministry team; the young solicitor, passionate about the gospel, who turned out to have an exceptional gift of service to the homeless—doing their washing, looking after their money and, above all, giving them hours and hours of her time; and the church administrator who was not only brilliant at organisation in the parish office but also exceptionally gifted at teaching in the pulpit.

CONCLUSION

We have seen that gospel ministry goes beyond bringing people to Christ and teaching them to lead faithful Christian lives; it also includes building a Christian community, which Paul called the body of Christ, where every member has a gift and a ministry. Christians are to use these gifts and ministries to serve others, for the building up of God's new community and for the glory of Christ. The gospel then becomes incarnated into a vibrant local church, where truth and grace can be seen and experienced, as well as taught and explained. This is the 'body beautiful' or, to change the metaphor, the bride of Christ, which is being prepared for the wonderful day when the bridegroom arrives. Christian leaders have been given the Word and the Spirit to help them with this glorious responsibility of preparing the bride.

Notes

1   Romans 12:3–8; 1 Corinthians 12:4–30; Ephesians 4:4–16; Colossians 1:18; see also David Watson, *I Believe in the Church* (Hodder, 1978), ch. 7

2   Rick Warren, *The Purpose Driven Church* (Zondervan, 1995), pp. 20–21

3   Bill Hybels, *Courageous Leadership* (Zondervan, 2002), p. 23

4   John Stott, *The Living Church* (IVP, 2007), pp.19–21

5   Nicky Gumbel, *Questions of Life* (Alpha/Kingsway, reprinted 2004), pp. 216–217

6   John Stott suggests something similar to this in *God's New Society* (IVP, 1979), p. 168.

7   Ephesians 4:15–16

8   1 Corinthians 12:12–13; Ephesians 4:4

9   1 Corinthians 12:4–6

10 Romans 12; 1 Corinthians 12; Ephesians 4; though not Colossians 1, because there he is emphasising the headship of Christ

11 Ephesians 4:13

12 Note that John Stott says, '"Charismatic" is not a term which can be accurately applied to any group or movement within the church, since according to the New Testament the whole church is a charismatic community. It is the body of Christ, every single member of which has a gift (*charisma*) to exercise or function to perform' (*God's New Society*, p. 156). At the end of this section he concludes, 'We have seen that it is the exalted Christ who bestows gifts on his church, that his gifts are very diverse in character, that the teaching gifts are

primary, and that their purpose is to equip God's people for their ministries and so build up Christ's body' (p. 168).

13 Please note Wayne Grudem's comment: 'There is a large "middle" group with respect to this question, a group of "mainstream evangelicals" who are neither charismatics or Pentecostals on the one hand, nor "cessationists" on the other.' (Wayne Grudem, *Systematic Theology*, IVP, reprinted 2007, p. 131). This view is classically expressed by John Woodhouse in *The Briefing* (April 2010, 'Where have all the miracles gone?').

14 See especially Grudem, *Systematic Theology* (pp. 1016–1047), Max Turner, *The Holy Spirit and Spiritual Gifts* (pp. 286–302), Jack Deere, *Surprised by the Power of the Spirit* (pp. 99–115), Simon Ponsonby, *God Inside Out* (pp. 255–280).

15 See, for example, Colossians 2:16–19.

16 Note John Stott here: 'What is certain is that, since neither Stephen nor Philip was an apostle, Scripture does not warrant a rigid restriction of miracles to the apostles' (*The Message of Acts*, IVP, p. 148).

17 See Galatians 3:5; 1 Corinthians 12:8–10

18 James 5:14–16

19 For example, see Jack Deere, *Surprised by the Power of the Spirit* (Kingsway, 1993, pp. 49–52, where he makes this point brilliantly.

20 See Chapter 3.

21 There are other historical reasons why they got separated. For a summary of these, see Ponsonby, *God Inside Out*, pp. 59–81. I also believe that the more extreme versions of the modern Charismatic movement are partly responsible for the separation. How can mainstream Evangelicalism identify with Charismatic renewal when prophetic revelations are taken more seriously than biblical revelation, when physical healing becomes more important than saving the lost, when shallow preaching replaces systematic Bible exposition, and when the Charismatic 'gospel' is more about 'God meeting our every need' than 'God demands all people everywhere to repent'? Tendencies like these have led to some very valid and searching critiques, for example, David Bebbington, *Evangelicalism in Modern Britain* (pp. 229–248), J.I. Packer, *Keep in Step with the Spirit* (pp. 191–199), or Stott, *God's New Society* (pp. 155–173).

22 Packer, *Keep in Step with the Spirit*, p. 188

23 Warren, *Purpose Driven Church*, p. 368

24 2 Timothy 3:15–17 (TNIV)

25 See Warren, *Purpose Driven Church*, pp. 369–375

26 Genesis 37—41

27 Matthew 16:13–28

28 2 Corinthians 12:7–10; Philippians 1:12–14

29 Dallas Willard, *The Divine Conspiracy* (Fount, 1998)

30 Timothy George, *Theology of the Reformers* (Broadman & Holman, 1988), p. 53

31 2 Corinthians 5:14–15

32 1 Corinthians 14:1, 12

33 1 Corinthians 12:29–30

34 1 Corinthians 12:14–20

35 For a much fuller treatment of the gifts of the Spirit, see Turner, *The Holy Spirit and Spiritual Gifts* (pp. 181–359), David Prior, *The Message of 1 Corinthians* (IVP, 1985, pp. 192–255), Grudem, *Systematic Theology* (pp. 1016–1084) or Williams, *Renewal Theology* (pp. 323–409).

36 Acts 1:8; Ephesians 5:18

37 2 Timothy 1:6

8

ENABLING WORSHIP AND PRAYER

There is no doubt that worship in the Bible encompasses the whole of life, with corporate worship being just the tip of the iceberg. Jesus summarised the Old Testament commandments by saying that you should 'Love the Lord your God with all your heart and with all your soul and with all your strength and with all your mind',[1] and he told the Samaritan woman that true worship in the new era of the kingdom was not about locations or temples but mind and heart ('in spirit and in truth').[2] Paul talked of our true worship being the laying down of our lives as 'living sacrifices'[3] and urged the Colossians, 'Whatever you do, whether in word or deed, do it all in the name of the Lord Jesus, giving thanks to God the Father through him.'[4] Learning to see our daily lives through God's eyes is part of our Christian calling, and aiming to bring God glory through our work, leisure, relationships, hopes and struggles is an act of worship. The Shorter Westminster Confession was right when it identified worship as our highest human calling: 'The chief end of man is to glorify God and to enjoy him for ever.' We were created for this!

Church leaders have a central role in helping people make connections between faith and life, so that all of life becomes an act of worship. John Pritchard, the Bishop of Oxford, talks about this role in terms of being 'a practical theologian, revealing and clarifying the connections between the things of God and the things of people's everyday experience'. He continues:

In some cases the connections are obvious and urgent. The death of a child leads us to reflect on suffering and theodicy; starting a healing ministry leads us to reflect on divine action; the invasion of a country in the Middle East leads us to re-examine just war theory; a new book by Richard Dawkins leads us to think about science and religion. At other times the connections are less pressing but they are the material out of which maturity of faith grows. How do we reflect theologically on the closure of a local factory? A Government White Paper on education, a cult television programme, or a national sporting triumph? How do we help people to connect their thinking about God to their life at work, their ambition and decisions in the workplace, the bringing up of their children, or the care of their father-in-law with dementia?[5]

WORD AND SPIRIT HELP US TO MAKE THESE IMPORTANT CONNECTIONS

The Bible is our greatest resource in helping us to think 'Christianly' about the world. John Stott made this point very powerfully in his book *Issues Facing Christians Today*, when he appealed to the Evangelical constituency to rediscover its mislaid social conscience and start to make connections between the Christian faith and the complex issues of our world. He called for Christians in general and church leaders in particular[6] to develop a worldview shaped by the fourfold scheme of biblical revelation (creation, fall, redemption and consummation). He wrote, 'This fourfold biblical reality... supplies the true perspective from which to view the unfolding process between two eternities, the vision of God working out his purposes. It gives us a framework into which to fit everything, a way of integrating our understanding, the possibility of thinking straight, even about the most complex issues.'[7] The consequence of this is that, as we teach the Bible systematically, we can help our congregation to integrate faith and life, and so let everything they do become an act of worship. The alternative is that we create a church full of people who think pious thoughts and express spiritual devotion on a Sunday, but who think and behave very differently during the week. Leaders *must* make those connections, and the Bible will help us to do that.

The Spirit is also available to help us prepare people to live lives of worship. At the end of the same chapter, Stott talks about three other gifts from God to help us. Alongside the Bible there is also the Holy Spirit (who opens the Scriptures to us and helps us to apply them), the human mind (being shaped by the Word and renewed by the Spirit) and the Christian community (living under the Word and indwelt by the Spirit).[8] From here flows a life of worship, enriched by the Holy Spirit's presence in the believer, bringing the fruit of the Spirit and obedience to Christ. For true worship is shown in a holy life, as Samuel spelt out to King Saul: 'To obey is better than sacrifice, and to heed is better than the fat of rams.' Jesus makes the same point to his disciples: 'If you love me, you will obey what I command.' Paul's command to be 'filled with the Spirit' comes in the context of an exhortation to 'live as children of light... and find out what pleases the Lord'.[9] A holy life is our deepest act of worship, and the Holy Spirit is the chief agent in our sanctification. For leaders, this cannot be emphasised strongly enough.[10] Robert Murray McCheyne, the 19th-century Scottish preacher, once said, 'The greatest need of my people is my personal holiness.'[11]

WORD AND SPIRIT IN ENABLING CORPORATE WORSHIP

Although Christian worship can be broadly defined as 'a life lived to the glory of God', there is, and always has been, a corporate dimension, which is what I called earlier 'the tip of the iceberg'. Throughout the Bible, God's people are encouraged to meet together to glorify his name, to celebrate his goodness, greatness and grace, to confess their sins, to hear his Word taught and applied, and to enjoy his holy and powerful presence. These are the reasons that God commanded the setting up of the tabernacle in the wilderness and the building of the temple in Jerusalem under the old covenant, and this corporate dimension continues on into the New Testament, as we see from the early Christian gatherings for worship.[12] Jesus redefines the true temple as his body, destroyed in three days and then rebuilt,[13] and his followers become the living stones 'being built into a spiritual house to be a holy priesthood, offering spiritual sacrifices to God through Jesus Christ'.[14] Just as God promised to come among his people in Old Testament times when they met in his name, so now, in the new covenant, Jesus comes among his people by his Spirit: 'For where two or three come together in my name, there am I with them.'[15] Like Moses at the burning bush, we stand on holy ground in times of worship, although, sadly, we often miss it. Here our risen Lord meets with us, speaks to us, exposes us, forgives us, reassures us, teaches us, feeds us, fills us and sends us out 'to live and work to his praise and glory'.[16]

As church leaders, it is our privilege to plan and oversee these times of corporate worship. Although members of the Church of England have different understandings of the word 'priest', ranging from the more sacerdotal catholic 'priest', representing Christ at the Eucharist, to the more functional reformed view of 'presbyter', the pastor and teacher of God's flock, all are agreed that we have the task of leading God's people in worship, preaching and teaching God's word and celebrating the sacraments of communion and baptism. Priests (presbyters) in the Church of England are instructed at their ordination 'to lead God's people in the offering of worship, offering with them a spiritual sacrifice of praise and thanksgiving'.[17] So Cocksworth and Brown, in their book exploring the true nature of the church leader's task, say:

Presbyters stand on holy ground, ground sanctified by God's presence. Their ministry is to serve this promise. Doing so extends far wider than what is done in the church building or even among the community of the church. It includes every opportunity for the opening of eyes and ears and hearts to the activity of God in the world. But it is concentrated in a liturgical ministry that 'proclaims the gospel of salvation' through a ministry of preaching and teaching, Eucharist and baptism.[18]

Similarly, Michael Sadgrove, the Dean of Durham, in a book that mines the depths of the Old Testament Wisdom literature for insight into the tasks of leadership and ministry, reflects on the Song of Songs and likens the church to 'a community of delight', discovering what it means to 'glorify God and enjoy him for ever'. He then highlights the role of the church leader: 'The ordained ministry of the church is the visible focus of all this... If we ask what is at the *heart* of priestly ministry, I reply that it is *to preside over the Church's praise of God*. The Church is never more a community of delight than when we offer our praises at the Eucharist.'[19]

The Bible has been given to us by God to aid us in this task. It is God's self-revelation; it is how he makes himself known to us. So if we want God to meet with his people, then the reading and exposition of the Bible has to have a central place. In Chapter 4 we saw that this means prayerful hard work and study during the week. It also means preaching the sermon as if our life depended on it, not just reading it or putting it across tentatively, but communicating it with conviction, clarity and passion as God's messenger bringing God's Word to God's people. Some of us may want to use the church's lectionary: it saves us having to choose our subjects and passages, and forces us to preach on parts of the Bible we might not have chosen. It also contains themes of Christian life and discipleship, as well as seasonal passages, so that we can be sure that we are preaching on Advent themes in Advent, and Lenten themes in Lent. Others will want to preach through books of the Bible in a systematic way. The great value of this kind of expository preaching is the way it allows us to get inside a part of Scripture and let it speak to us on its own terms. Over a few weeks, a particular Bible book becomes familiar: we grasp its context, we listen to its message and we receive its challenge. The book becomes our friend and companion for the journey through life. It becomes part of our spiritual DNA, shaping the way we live and drawing us into worship.

At other times we will need to do some thematic preaching, such as 'Bible characters', 'Christian stewardship' or 'What would

Jesus say to Richard Dawkins, or David Cameron, or Jonathan Ross?' One year we did four sermons on church history, using four Bible themes: how the Church has grown and spread over the years, how the Church has suffered persecution, how the Church has defended the faith against false teaching, and how the Church has experienced revival and renewal. I also did four sermons on 'The story of the Bible', using the key biblical figures whom God used at different times: Genesis to Psalms, Proverbs to Malachi, the Gospels, and Acts to Revelation.

In addition to preaching, the Bible needs to permeate the whole service. I usually started a service with a sentence from Scripture, we would make sure that our songs of worship were based on scriptural truths, we led into the confession with a reminder of God's laws and commandments, we trained our lesson readers to read the Bible with clarity and confidence, we let the Bible explain the meaning of the baptism and Communion, we used the Bible to test any prophetic words or pictures, and we used biblical exhortations to challenge people to respond to God.[20] Having the Bible as our reference point in everything ensures that we are worshipping the true and living God, who has revealed himself in Jesus Christ and who comes among us by his Spirit.

The Spirit is also able to help us in our services of worship. He brings Christ's presence to us, making true the promise of Jesus that he will be in our midst when we meet in his name.[21] Of course the Holy Spirit lives in our hearts all the time, but there is something very special about the gathering of God's people, when we become the living temple which God indwells by his Spirit.[22] More than that, the Spirit reveals the glory of Christ. The apostle John was 'in the Spirit on the Lord's day' when he had that wonderful vision of Christ in Revelation 1:12–18. We too will be able to glimpse the glory and grace of Christ through the worship, the preaching and the Eucharist, because the Spirit's work is to reveal him to us.[23] He also leads us into worship, praise and thanksgiving.[24] The sung worship is not the product of the worship band or the choir, although they have their part to play in facilitating the worship;

it is, rather, the overflow of lives filled with the Spirit and deeply grateful for our salvation.

Another dimension of the Spirit's work is that he convicts us of our sins and, through our corporate confession, will bring forgiveness, grace and greater wholeness, reassuring us of the Father's love and pouring God's love into our hearts all over again.[25] The Spirit also teaches us from the Scriptures and equips us for Christian living and service,[26] as we have seen in Chapter 4, and builds up the Church through the exercise of gifts,[27] as we saw in Chapter 7. He enlivens the sacraments of baptism and the Eucharist, as was the experience of the first disciples following the outpouring of the Holy Spirit on the day of Pentecost.[28] Holy Communion becomes a powerful reminder of Christ's sacrifice for us, and we are enabled to 'feed on him in our hearts by faith with thanksgiving'.[29] This is why there is an invocation to the Holy Spirit in many of the eucharistic prayers.[30] Similarly, baptism becomes an effective sign when the Spirit brings to life what the sacrament promises.[31] As we enjoy our fellowship together in the Holy Spirit, he encourages and challenges us through our fellow Christians.[32] Finally, he empowers and direct the Church's mission in our times of corporate worship,[33] and convicts unbelievers,[34] bringing them to Christ.[35] John Leech, in his book *Liturgy and Liberty*, provides a liturgical framework (or worship cycle) for the activity of the Spirit in all of these ways, drawing worshippers into a deeper devotion and submission to Christ.[36]

John Stott's definition of 'spiritual worship' in *The Living Church* brings together Word, Worship and Sacrament, and highlights the double need for the objective truth of the Scriptures and the subjective experience of the living Jesus present among his people:

What is needed, then? Firstly, we need such a faithful reading and preaching of God's word that through it his living voice is heard addressing his people again. Secondly, we need a reverent and expectant administration of the Eucharist or Lord's Supper that (I choose my words carefully) there is a Real Presence of Jesus Christ… not in the elements, but among his people... so that we may feed on him in our hearts by faith. Thirdly, we need such a sincere offering of praise and prayer, that God's people say with Jacob 'Surely the Lord is in this place, and I was not aware of it' (Genesis 28:16), and unbelievers fall down and worship God exclaiming 'God is really among you!' (1 Corinthians 14:24–25).[37]

THE STRATEGIC IMPORTANCE OF PRAYER

There is a fascinating story in Exodus 17:8–16, where the Israelites have come out of Egypt through the Red Sea and have entered the Sinai desert. Almost immediately the Amalekites come and attack them. Moses says to Joshua, 'Choose some of our men and go out to fight the Amalekites. Tomorrow I will stand on top of the hill with the staff of God in my hands' (v. 9). 'As long as Moses held up his hands, the Israelites were winning, but whenever he lowered his hands, the Amalekites were winning' (v. 11). So important were the prayers of Moses that when his arms grew tired, Aaron and Hur made him sit down on a stone, and they each held up his hands on either side. Consequently the Israelites won a great victory, and Moses built an altar there and called it 'The Lord is my Banner... for hands were lifted up to the throne of the Lord' (vv. 15–16).

Now I think that story is more than an illustration of the power of prayer. I think it establishes the principle, early on in the life of God's people, that God's kingdom rule is established through prayer. When the hands of God's people are up and calling out to God, his purposes are accomplished, but when hands come down and prayer flags, things don't happen and the church doesn't move forward. I can't fully understand that, because I believe that God is sovereign and that he can do whatever he wants, independently of us; but what I do know, because I see it in Scripture and in church history, is that God moves powerfully in answer to prayer, as his people cry out to him and say, 'Your kingdom come, your will be done on earth as it is in heaven.'[38] The Lord's Prayer is merely reiterating this point.

Jesus taught his disciples that 'apart from me you can do nothing',[39] and, although we often think of that verse individualistically, it is more likely that Jesus was meaning it corporately. The local church can't achieve anything unless it abides in Christ and stays connected to him as branches to the vine. This would explain Paul's constant refrain to the newly formed churches of Asia Minor to 'pray continually', to 'pray in the Spirit on all occasions with all kinds of prayers and requests', and to 'have no anxiety about anything, but in everything by prayer and supplication with thanksgiving let your requests be made known to God'.[40] So, in local churches, we must keep our hands lifted up to God in humble dependence on him if we are to see the kingdom grow in the communities and parishes where we serve, and the powers of darkness defeated.[41] These are the spiritual dynamics of the kingdom: God establishes his rule on earth through the saving work of Christ, as the Holy Spirit moves in answer to the prayers of God's people. The church prayer meeting is still the powerhouse behind the church's ministry, and leaders need to think of imaginative ways of reinventing it.

It is worth reminding ourselves that the 18th-century Evangelical awakening in England began as the result of a prayer meeting. A traditional Moravian 'Watch Night' service on New Year's Eve, 1738, in Fetter Lane, London, began with 60 people gathering for a fellowship meal as a prelude to Communion.

None could imagine the profound effect that night would have on the world... As the evening passed and the morning of the first day of the New Year began, the group began praying. As they continued praying together, Wesley records,[42] 'the power of God came mightily upon' the group [at] about three in the morning. Some fell to the ground, awestruck and overwhelmed at the very presence of God. Others were filled with 'exceeding joy' as they experienced the presence of God. All were caught by surprise, but when they recovered somewhat, they united their voices to sing a hymn: 'We praise thee, O God, we acknowledge Thee to be the Lord'. The Evangelical Revival, as it came to be called in England, had begun.[43]

John and Charles Wesley and George Whitfield were all present that evening; it launched them into their ministries, and so impacted the entire nation, not to mention the North American continent, for Christ.

Billy Graham believed that prayer lay behind the extraordinary events in London during his visit in 1954, when the Harringay Arena was filled to capacity night after night, and 120,000 people gathered for the final service at Wembley Stadium. Thousands gave their lives to Christ and, when he returned to London for another mission in 1966, 52 Anglican clergymen sat on the platform with him who had all been first won for Christ at Harringay. Why such an impact? Graham believed it was because 800 people spent the night in prayer just before the mission began, and prayer groups around the world were focusing their attention on London at that time. Graham had three secrets to revival: prayer, prayer and prayer.[44] Historians of revivals would agree: 'The most constant of all factors which appear in revivals is that of *urgent and persistent prayer*. The fact is acknowledged by all writers on the subject.'[45]

WORD AND SPIRIT ENABLING PRAYER

The Bible is a wonderful resource to us as leaders as we enable our churches to pray. Firstly, it commands us to pray,[46] so the call to prayer comes from God himself rather than just the minister. Also, it teaches us how to pray,[47] so we have a handbook of God's wisdom on how to do it, including many examples of God's people at prayer,[48] with plenty of inspiring material to motivate people. It also contains some of the finest prayers ever prayed, including the Lord's Prayer,[49] so we can learn from them about what we should pray for. In addition to this, it contains many wonderful promises about God's willingness to hear and answer our prayers,[50] and shows us that we can pray at all times,[51] not only when we are rejoicing and full of thanks and praise but also when we are suffering and experiencing real pain and struggle. Looking back over my preaching during the past 25 years, I can't find a year when I didn't teach on some aspects of prayer, either through sermon series like 'People in prayer' or 'The great prayers of the Bible', or addressing the subject as we worked through one of the biblical books. Inevitably the Bible did its work, and the Spirit used the Word to challenge people to pray.

The Spirit will also help us actually to pray. Teaching on prayer is so important, but it is only the first stage of real intimacy with God. Writing to the Romans, Paul said, 'The Spirit helps us in our weakness. We do not know what we ought to pray for, but the Spirit himself intercedes for us with groans that words cannot express.'[52] Philip Yancey, in his honest and helpful book *Prayer: Does It Make Any Difference?*, comments on this verse in Romans and says, 'Christ's Spirit is praying within us even when we lack both the wisdom and the words for prayer... Though we feel ignorant in our prayers, the Spirit does not. Though we feel exhausted and confused, the Spirit does not. Though we feel lacking in faith, the Spirit does not... We need only groan—and attend to a presence already there.'[53] I am quite sure that this is why Paul encourages us to 'pray in the Spirit on all occasions',[54] for the Spirit helps us to know the mind of Christ and to pray according to his will.

Michael Green wrote a searching challenge to local churches, theological colleges and ordinary Christians in his book *On Your Knees! St Paul at Prayer*. He had experienced the passionate praying of Christians from the developing world and then compared it with the shallow, superficial praying of the church in the Western world:

This is an area where we in the West are weak. Rationalistic children of the Enlightenment that we are, we are convinced at gut level that it is our intellect rather than our prayers that is critical for success in life. The churches believe this, with an accent on programme rather than prayer. The theological colleges believe this, with an accent on theory rather than on prayer. The ordinary everyday Christian believes this, with only a very few moments spent in prayer each day. This shows where our priorities lie. We do not have because we do not ask, as James put it succinctly in his letter (James 4:2). Is it any wonder that we see so little of the power of God, compared to our prayer-conscious brothers and sisters in Korea and Singapore, in Sao Paulo and Dar es Salaam? They know that prayer is the pathway to power. And we, frankly, do not believe it.[55]

Despite many stirrings to pray,[56] I think most of us still need to hear this, not least those of us working in theological colleges and training tomorrow's church leaders.

WORD AND SPIRIT IN MEETING OUR SPIRITUAL HUNGER AND THIRST FOR GOD

As Christian leaders, should we hunger and thirst after God? Some might say 'No!' on the grounds that, in Christ, all our spiritual hunger and thirst has been satisfied. Isn't this what Jesus promised in John 6:35 and 7:37–38? How could we doubt his Word by still claiming to be spiritually hungry and thirsty? Isn't the same mistake made by those who seek additional 'spiritual blessings' when we have already been given 'every spiritual blessing in Christ'?[57] The idea of wanting 'more' seems almost blasphemous!

I understand the point entirely and believe it captures the fundamental biblical truth about the sufficiency of Christ as Saviour, Lord and Friend. He is everything we need and 'in him are hidden all the treasures of wisdom and knowledge'.[58] To come to faith in him is to trust our lives into the hands of all-sufficient Saviour, 'in whom all our hungers are satisfied'.[59]

However, there is a danger of overplaying this gospel truth, because it then creates three insurmountable problems. Firstly, and most importantly, it obliterates those biblical passages that talk about an ongoing longing by God's people to know and experience him at a deeper level.[60] It is important to note that many of them are in the New Testament, so we can't argue that this longing to know God better was simply an Old Testament hope, which has now been fulfilled in Christ. How can we possibly preach on these passages if we don't believe that Christians should now be having any spiritual hunger or thirst for God? Secondly, it requires us to dismiss 2000 years of Christian spirituality. What are we to make of the experience of Christians throughout the centuries, from the Desert Fathers, the monastics and the Puritans to those who have attended the Keswick Convention, Spring Harvest and New Wine, who all describe a longing for a deeper intimacy and closeness to the Lord? Were they all pitifully misguided? Thirdly, it demands an extraordinary amount of self-delusion. Are you as close to the Lord as you could be? Does your prayer life have no room for improvement? Have you never lost your first love of Christ? Has sin never robbed you of your intimacy with the Lord? Has suffering never driven you into a spiritual desert? Are you always filled with the Holy Spirit? If all your answers are 'Yes', then you are proving my point about being self-deluded![61]

Martyn Lloyd-Jones thundered at his congregation in Westminster Chapel in a sermon on 25 May 1961 when he detected a spiritual self-contentedness and lack of hunger for a deeper experience of God: 'Got it all? I simply ask in the name of God, why then are you as you are? If you have got it all, why are you so unlike the New Testament Christians? Got it all? Got it all at your conversion? Well, where is it, I ask?!'[62] I'm glad I wasn't in the chapel that evening when the great doctor challenged his flock out of their spiritual complacency!

Is there a way of holding together these two important biblical truths of spiritual satisfaction and spiritual hunger? I believe so. In becoming Christians, we have been adopted out of spiritual poverty into God's family, and all the rights and privileges of being sons and daughters of God are now ours through Christ. Our long-term inheritance is secure, and our day-to-day provision is always there. But we still need to grow in our faith and become mature in Christ, and this is why we get spiritually hungry and thirsty (in a way that parallels human growth). Our spiritual hunger and thirst are met mostly on a day-to-day basis through prayer, and studying the Scriptures, and weekly nurturing through our local church, but sometimes we have longer periods of time, often caused by sinful behaviour or painful suffering, when we feel a holy discontentment with our spiritual progress for a variety of reasons and we long for a deeper experience and knowledge of God. We begin to seek him with fresh earnestness, sometimes with prayer and fasting, and God graciously provides for our needs. A wonderful biblical example of this provision is the way God looked after Elijah through the very dark and difficult times in his ministry, and restored his soul in exactly the way Psalm 23 would later describe.[63] Another would be Paul's struggles with his 'thorn in the flesh', and the way he was shown that God's grace was sufficient for him and God's power was made perfect in his weakness.[64]

How does God do this work of nurture and restoration? How does he satisfy those who hunger and thirst for righteousness? How does he renew and deepen our love for Christ? I am sure there are lots of ways, and we would be wise to dig deep into the wells of Christian spirituality.[65] Yet the primary means of restoration have to be his Word and his Spirit: his Word is our spiritual food and daily bread[66] and his Spirit is our spiritual drink and life-giving spring.[67] These are our two primary sources of spiritual refreshment and renewal, because both of them lead us back into a deeper love for Christ and into the warmth and intimacy of the Father's embrace.

CONCLUSION

This chapter has looked at how we, as church leaders, can help our people to 'glorify God and enjoy him for ever'. I have suggested that the Word of God and the Spirit of God are our two greatest resources for this task, remembering that both of them point away from themselves to Christ. Jesus is glorified and exalted in our worship, our prayers and our spiritual hunger and thirst when the Word and the Spirit are allowed to exercise their complementary and overlapping ministries. Paul's command to 'let the Holy Spirit fill you' is paralleled in a very similar passage by 'let the word of Christ dwell in you richly'.[68]

Notes

1 Luke 10:27
2 John 4:21–24
3 Romans 12:1
4 Colossians 3:17
5 John Pritchard, *The Life and Work of a Priest* (SPCK, 2007), pp. 50–51
6 Note his 'Call for Christian leadership' in John Stott, *Issues Facing Christians Today* (Zondervan, 4th edition revised 2006), ch. 17.
7 Stott, *Issues Facing Christians Today*, p. 64
8 Stott, *Issues Facing Christians Today*, p. 70
9 1 Samuel 15:22; John 14:15; Ephesians 5:8–18
10 Jonathan Lamb's *Integrity—Leading with God Watching* (IVP, 2006) emphasises this powerfully.
11 http://web.ukonline.co.uk/d.haslam/mccheyne/cheadle/RMMCSSDFH.PDF
12 See Acts 2:42–47; Colossians 3:15–17; Ephesians 5:18–20; 1 Corinthians 14:26–33
13 Mark 14:58
14 1 Peter 2:5
15 1 Kings 6:11–14; Matthew 18:20
16 Part of the Prayer of Dismissal in the *Common Worship* Eucharist
17 From *Common Worship*: The Ordination of Priests, also called Presbyters
18 Christopher Cocksworth and Rosalind Brown, *Being a Priest Today* (Canterbury Press, 2nd edition 2006), p. 64
19 Michael Sadgrove, *Wisdom and Ministry: The call to leadership* (SPCK, 2008), pp. 128–129
20 See Isaiah 55:6; Matthew 11:28; Hebrews 3:7–8
21 Matthew 18:20
22 Ephesians 2:22; 1 Peter 2:5
23 John 16:14
24 Ephesians 5:18–20
25 John 16:8; 1 John 1:8–9; 2 Corinthians 3:17–18; Galatians 4:6–7; Romans 5:8
26 2 Timothy 3:16—4:2
27 1 Corinthians 14:26
28 Acts 2:41–42

29 Invitation to Communion, *Common Worship*, p. 180
30 Invitation to Communion, *Common Worship*, pp. 184–201, for example, 'Send the Holy Spirit on your people' (B), 'Send your Spirit on us now' (D), 'Pour out your Holy Spirit' (G).
31 See the Prayer over the Water, *Common Worship*, p. 355.
32 2 Corinthians 13:14; Hebrews 10:24
33 Acts 1:8; 13:2
34 Acts 2:37–41; 1 Corinthians 14:24–25
35 It is worth noting that most of these biblical references are written in the plural context of church communities.
36 A revised and updated version is *Living Liturgy* (Kingsway, 1997).
37 John Stott, *The Living Church*, p. 46
38 Matthew 6:10
39 John 15:5
40 1 Thessalonians 5:17; Ephesians 6:18; Philippians 4:6 (RSV)
41 2 Corinthians 10:4
42 Recorded in John Wesley's journal (1927:3839)
43 E. Towns and D. Porter, *The Ten Greatest Revivals Ever* (Vine, 2000), p. 66
44 Nicky Gumbel, *The Heart of Revival* (Kingsway, 1997), p. 186
45 R.E. Davies, *I Will Pour Out My Spirit* (Monarch, 1992), p. 217
46 For example, Romans 12:12
47 For example, Luke 11:1–14
48 For example, 1 Chronicles 29:10–20
49 For example, Matthew 6:5–13
50 For example, Matthew 7:7–11
51 For example, 1 Thessalonians 5:17–18
52 Romans 8:26
53 Philip Yancey, *Prayer: Does It Make Any Difference?* (Hodder, 2006), p. 102
54 Ephesians 6:18
55 Michael Green, *On Your Knees! St Paul at Prayer* (Eagle, 1992), p. 40
56 See Charlie Cleverly, *The Discipline of Intimacy* (Kingsway, 2002), pp. 17–19
57 Ephesians 1:3
58 John 6:67–69; Colossians 2:3
59 Eucharist Prayer, *Common Worship*
60 For example, Psalm 42:1–3; 51:9–11; 84:1–12; Lamentations 3:13–24; Isaiah 40:27–31; John 21:15–17; Ephesians 1:14; 3:14–21; 2 Peter 3:18; Revelation 2:1–7; 3:14–22
61 Much fuller arguments for pursuing a deeper experience of God can be found in Simon Ponsonby, *More: How you can have more of the Spirit when you have everything in Christ* (Victor, 2004) and John Piper, *Desiring God: The pathway to spiritual growth* (Hodder, 2008 edition).

62 Sermon on 'Baptism in the Spirit', 25 May 1961. I think Lloyd Jones was describing a real, subsequent experience of the Holy Spirit to which millions of Christians can testify, but almost definitely using the wrong terminology. To me, the biblical data points to 'baptism in the Spirit' as being part of Christian initiation, and subsequent experiences are best described as 'being filled with the Spirit' or 'being renewed by the Spirit'. But changing the terminology is not a reason for missing out on the experience(s) that he was encouraging!

63 1 Kings 17—19; Psalm 23

64 2 Corinthians 12:1–10

65 See, for example, Richard Foster, *Streams of Living Water: Celebrating the great traditions of the Christian faith* (HarperCollins, 1999) or *Celebration of Discipline: The pathway to spiritual growth* (Hodder, 2008 Edition).

66 Psalm 119:103; Jeremiah 15:16; Matthew 4:4; Acts 20:32; 1 Corinthians 3:2; 1 Peter 2:2

67 Isaiah 55:1; Ezekiel 36:25–26; John 4:13–14; 7:37–39; 1 Corinthians 12:13; Ephesians 5:18

68 Ephesians 5:18 (NEB); Colossians 3:16 (NEB); as highlighted by Stott, *God's New Society*, p. 209

PROVIDING PASTORAL CARE
AND NURTURE

Some years ago, a friend of mine was visiting King's College Chapel, Cambridge, and was shocked to see that the altarpiece, the famous Rubens painting *Adoration of the Magi*, had been vandalised by a terrorist group who had scratched their initials across the picture.[1] While he was processing this devastating news and feeling very sad that such a beautiful masterpiece should have been ruined, his eyes dropped to a little notice underneath the picture, which simply said, 'It is believed that this painting can be restored.' My friend's heart missed a beat with joy and relief: there was hope for the painting despite the damage. It has now been beautifully restored.

Something similar happens with our lives. We are all masterpieces of God's creation, 'fearfully and wonderfully made', in the words of the psalmist,[2] but sin may have so spoilt our lives that we are hardly recognisable as creatures made in the image of God. Then, just when we think all is lost, we encounter the joyful and liberating news of the gospel. Through the saving death and resurrection of Jesus Christ, there is hope for our broken lives to be made new, and the image of God can be restored within us. The work of pastoral care and nurture plays a key part in this restoration process.

THE ENORMOUS PRIVILEGE OF PASTORAL MINISTRY

All too often, people assume that Christian leaders live inside spiritual ivory towers, protected from the harsh realities of life by a world of church, services and saintly people. I would say that precisely the opposite is the case! The very nature of our job takes us into the complex and painful situations of people's lives in an unprecedented way (arguably more so than any other profession). I've sat alongside a young couple and held their newborn baby as he has been dying of a congenital disease. I've taken the funeral service of a notorious armed robber and done my best to comfort the grieving family. I've prayed in the homes of families that have been troubled with an evil presence. I've hugged couples going through the painful nightmare of marriage breakdown and divorce. I've listened to the stories of people who are being made unexpectedly redundant, or who remain unemployed after numerous job applications. I've prayed with those addicted to drugs and alcohol or broken by child abuse or domestic violence, and spent time listening to the tragic stories of the homeless. Ivory tower? Not in my experience of ministry. Although it has been hugely stretching and emotionally exhausting, it has also been an enormous privilege and one that I am so grateful to God for.

Jesus the good shepherd

Jesus didn't stand aloof from situations of pastoral pain. He had a reputation for spending time with the broken and the outcasts, the sick and suffering. Yes, he nurtured and taught the disciples, training and equipping them to serve others when he returned to the Father.[3] Yes, he challenged the comfortable and exposed the hypocrites.[4] Yet much of his public ministry was directed towards those who had been damaged by the rough edges of life: the lepers, the beggars, the possessed, the lonely, the sexually immoral and the socially unacceptable. The way he touched their lives was not only an expression of the tender love and compassion of God, but also a tangible sign that the kingdom of God was arriving in his own life and ministry.[5] In this kingdom there is sight for the blind, health for the sick, forgiveness for the sinners, freedom for the oppressed and wholeness for the broken.[6] The effects of the fall are being undone: Christ is making all things new.[7]

BIBLICAL IMAGES OF PASTORING GOD'S PEOPLE

Throughout Scripture, we see God's leaders receiving pastoral authority and oversight to shepherd God's flock. Many excellent biblical studies have highlighted the connection between the pastoral imagery of shepherding and the task of Christian leadership today. Two in particular stand out in my mind: Derek Tidball's *Skilful Shepherds: Explorations in Pastoral Theology*[8] and Timothy Laniak's *Shepherds after My Own Heart: Pastoral Traditions and Leadership in the Bible*.[9] Both these studies emphasise that the shepherd's role of pastoral care goes beyond caring, listening and supporting people who are experiencing difficulties; it includes concepts of leadership (offering vision, guidance and discipline), nurture (feeding with God's Word and training in discipleship) and protection (guarding against false teachers and erroneous teaching), so that God's people grow to become mature in Christ[10] and effective servants of the gospel.[11]

John Stott's favourite designation of the Christian minister has always been that of 'the pastor', and in his book *The Contemporary Christian* he spells out seven ways in which a good pastor models himself on the good shepherd, Jesus, based on John 10:1–16. Stott concludes:

Here then is the beautiful idea of pastoral ministry which Jesus painted. Wherever there are sheep, whether lost or found, there is a need for pastors to seek and to shepherd them. Following the example of the good shepherd himself, human pastors will endeavour to know and serve, to lead, feed and rule the sheep of Christ's flock, to guard them from marauding wolves and to seek them when they have gone astray. And then, however little they may have been recognised, appreciated or honoured on earth... they will receive from the Chief Shepherd, when he appears, 'the crown of glory that will never fade away' (1 Peter 5:4).[12]

Similarly, John Hughes, in his book *The Pastor's Notebook*, speaks movingly about the shepherding role of pastors today: 'The function of leaders is to care for the spiritual welfare of the flock, to give them the nourishment they need for growth and development, to equip them for the work of mission, and to seek the lost, to restore and integrate them into the fold.'[13]

The Puritan divine Richard Baxter based his book *The Reformed Pastor* on Paul's charge to the Ephesian elders in Acts 20:28: 'Keep watch over yourselves and all the flock of which the Holy Spirit has made you overseers. Be shepherds of the church of God, which he bought with his own blood.' Baxter pleaded with fellow pastors:

Oh then, let us hear these arguments of Christ, whenever we feel ourselves grow dull or careless: Did I die for them, and will you not look after them? Were they worth my blood, and are they not worth your labour? Did I come down from heaven to earth, to seek and to save that which was lost, and will you not go to the next door, or street or village to seek them? How small is your labour and condescension to mine! I debased myself to this, but it is your honour to be so employed. Have I done and suffered so much for my salvation; and was I willing to make you a co-worker with me, and will you refuse what little lies in your hands?[14]

Sharing our pastoral responsibility with other leaders

Who should do this work? As we have already seen, in Exodus 18 Moses is so overburdened with the pastoral problems of the Israelites that God prompts Jethro to tell him to appoint judges who can help him, making his pastoral load lighter. They prove to be a great blessing to all concerned, not least to Moses. And in the New Testament, church leadership is always plural,[15] so the pastor is given a group of elders/overseers/deacons who share the weight of pastoral responsibilities.[16]

I have always looked for mature, godly people to help pastor the churches where I have served. I have found it important, for example, to appoint home group leaders who understand their pastoral responsibilities, a pastoral team to visit the sick, the elderly and the housebound, and a prayer ministry team. It can be really helpful to have teams to help with preparation for weddings and baptisms, and another to visit the bereaved. I have also valued Christian counsellors (usually based outside our own church) to whom more serious cases can be referred. All these people helped us meet the growing pastoral needs of those connected to the church as well as those who turned up and requested support. Acts 6:1–7 is a constant reminder to us to make sure that the 'ministry of the word and prayer' is our primary focus, and that we don't neglect our teaching and praying by being overwhelmed with pastoral problems. It is here that we need to remind ourselves of the wider roles of shepherding God's flock (leadership, nurture and protection as well as caring and supporting).

Having said that, we are still called to be the senior pastors of the flock and we cannot bypass our pastoral calling. Wallace Benn, in his commendation of the Baxter model of pastoral ministry, has written, 'Too many preachers do not like people, and remain aloof from people... but, as Baxter said, how will we preach effectively if we do not know the real joys and problems of our brothers and sisters?' [17]

So I believe there are still pastoral situations that we cannot and should not avoid. These would include visiting the sick and people who are dying in hospital, supporting those going through a major crisis, giving Communion to the elderly and housebound, helping with the preparation of those getting married or baptised, visiting the bereaved, praying with those who are experiencing spiritual oppression, visiting prisoners and supporting the vulnerable (especially the homeless and those with mental health issues). All this needs to be done alongside others, and with their help and support. Yet we can't abdicate these responsibilities without a serious neglect of our calling.

We also need to support and encourage our pastoral teams

and home group leaders. I would always try to attend the team leaders' meetings, not only so that I could be fully up to date on pastoral situations but so that I could show my appreciation of their ministry by my presence, interest and encouragement.

THE PASTORAL MINISTRY OF THE WHOLE CHURCH

It is also worth remembering that every Christian has pastoral responsibilities, in that we are all called to demonstrate Jesus' unconditional love for everybody. The answer to Cain's question in Genesis 4:9, 'Am I my brother's keeper?', is definitely 'Yes!' This comes through in much of Jesus' teaching: in the Sermon on the Mount, in the parables of the good Samaritan and the sheep and goats, and in his great commission to teach all that he has commanded.[18]

Paul exhorts the Christians at Rome, 'Rejoice with those who rejoice; mourn with those who mourn.'[19] He says to the Galatians, 'Bear one another's burdens, and so fulfil the law of Christ.'[20] What is the law of Christ? 'That you love one another as I have loved you.'[21] And in John's first epistle, he writes, 'This is how we know what love is: Jesus Christ laid down his life for us. And we ought to lay down our lives for our brothers.'[22] In other words, all Christians have been given the pastoral care of others, whether it be towards people in our church, workplace or neighbourhood. We mustn't walk by on the other side.

Therefore, as Christian leaders, we need to be clear about our role, avoiding two extremes. One extreme is to feel responsible for everyone's problems in the church and feel totally overwhelmed (and a complete failure because we can't sort everybody out). The other extreme is to say, 'Pastoral care is not my gift and it's not my ministry. Let other people do it. I'm going to concentrate on preaching the Bible and conducting public worship.' I fear we will not win the respect of our congregations if we go to either extreme. Yes, our job is 'to equip the saints for the work of ministry',[23] but one of the ministries mentioned in the previous verse—which God has given to the church—is the work of *the pastor*, and that word has all the shepherding connotations of loving and caring for our flock.

ALLOWING GOD TO WORK THROUGH THE BIBLE

Almost every book of the Bible was written in response to some pastoral situation, whether it is the book of Job, wrestling with the issue of unjust suffering, or Isaiah explaining why the Babylonian exile happened and what hope God offers for the future.[24] In the New Testament, Luke writes his story of Jesus with particular concerns in mind that were emerging in the early church (such as the inclusion of the Gentiles, the place of women in the kingdom, and the role of the Holy Spirit). Paul, in his epistles, is either sorting out the pastoral mess at Corinth or challenging the false teachers at Galatia, or answering questions about the timetable of the second coming at Thessalonica. The book of Revelation was written to support Christians going through the fires of Roman persecution, and the seven letters in chapters 2 and 3 addressed particular pastoral situations in the churches of Asia Minor.[25]

So how can we, as Christian leaders, allow the Bible to do its work of addressing the pastoral needs of the people who are connected with our churches? I would suggest three ways.

Firstly, we can address pastoral issues in our preaching and teaching. Expounding Haggai, for example, can involve tackling issues of half-heartedness and loss of spiritual focus. Expounding Corinthians can address issues as diverse as rivalry and division among Christians, on the one hand, and sexual purity and promiscuity on the other. I remember doing a series of sermons on pastoral issues entitled 'Dealing with...' anger, pride, lust, jealousy and so on. The sermon on 'Dealing with abuse' struck a particularly painful chord with one member of the congregation who came to see me afterwards. She said, 'I didn't realise that what happened to me as a child was technically abuse. Now I understand why it was so painful to handle. Please can I have some prayer?' God's Word has done its work in her life and brought to the surface a deep-rooted issue that needed dealing with, and (consequently) enabled her to enter into more of the fullness of life that Jesus had in store for her. I remember another sermon series when we looked at a whole range of social and moral issues from a biblical perspective. The one on gambling spoke powerfully to someone who was addicted to playing the National Lottery. 'It is time to stop,' she said to me afterwards. God's Word had proved sharper than a double-edged sword.[26]

Secondly, we can encourage and resource Bible studies in home groups. Small group meetings are a perfect opportunity for pastoral issues to be raised, so we need to help our home group leaders to allow this to happen. Inevitably, issues will surface and God's wisdom and good purposes can be discovered through the careful study of God's Word. For example, a series of studies on the life of Joseph (Genesis 37—50) can be used to bring up issues of unjust suffering and God's providential care. A carefully prepared study will ask the right questions and help the group to connect with the profound truth of Romans 8:28: 'In all things God works for the good of those who love him, who have been called according to his purpose.'

Thirdly, we can read a part of Scripture during our pastoral visits: Psalm 121 for someone going through a difficult crisis, Psalm 23 at the hospital bedside of someone who is critically ill, Joshua 1:1–10 for someone embarking on a new chapter in their lives, Philippians 4:5–6 for someone who is troubled and fearful, Romans 12:17–21 for people experiencing opposition or persecution, John 14:1–6 with a bereaved family. Even though it was written so long ago (and issues of context and culture must be taken seriously for God's authentic Word to be heard), the Bible still has an amazing relevance to our lives today. It speaks directly into our pastoral dilemmas. For example, I remember times when I have read Psalm 23 to the dying and witnessed the visible blessing it brought: sometimes the dying person was unable to say anything, but they heard the words and the slightest nod or twinkle in their eye indicated that the good shepherd had ministered his grace to them. During a baptism visit with a family who are not church attenders, there is always surprise when they realise Jesus' attitude to children, as shown in Luke 18:15–17, and how much we can learn from a child's simple, trusting attitude about entering the kingdom of heaven.

ALLOWING GOD TO WORK THROUGH THE SPIRIT

God's Spirit, in addition to using the Bible, will help us in the practice of our pastoral work. The passage that describes Jesus' ministry to the poor, the prisoners, the blind and the oppressed begins, 'The Spirit of the Lord is on me, because he has anointed me to...'[27] This anointing of the Holy Spirit was more than God's way of identifying Jesus as the Messiah; it was also God's equipping of his Son to do the works of the kingdom. This is why the Spirit descended on him at his baptism in the River Jordan: not simply as an identification of his divine Sonship but also as an empowering for his future ministry. He would do the works of the kingdom in the power and strength of God.

The same can be said of our ministry of pastoral care and nurture. The sending of the Spirit at Pentecost was more than a sign that Jesus' followers belonged to the people of God: it was God's wonderful equipping of his church with all the resources that they needed to fulfil the great commission: 'You will receive power when the Holy Spirit comes on you.'[28] This commission involved preaching the gospel *and* discipling new converts, so that the kingdom of God would come on earth as it is in heaven. Church leaders, in particular, need the anointing and power of the Holy Spirit for this work, because it is complex, endless and exhausting. The longer I was involved in parish ministry, the more I knew that I needed all the resources that God had made available.

We cannot (and were not meant to) do this kingdom work in our own strength: after all, even Paul was powerfully aware of this enabling strength for his ministry.[29]

Consider, too, the work of the Spirit in those to whom we are ministering. God's Spirit is given to all believers not only as the sign and seal of salvation but as the agent for sanctification and growth into Christian maturity and wholeness.[30] God fully intends to continue the good work he has begun in us, and bring it to completion at the day of Christ.[31] When we are offering pastoral care and nurture to those in our care, God is doing a deeper and transforming work by his Spirit. Roger Hurding, in his book *Restoring the Image*, talks about the vital work of the Spirit in relation to our pastoral care and counselling:

Can we be changed? The Bible tells us loud and clear that we can be! Our... basic personalities, or in the biblical language our 'old nature', are distorted, incomplete and sinful without Christ. By the nurture of the Holy Spirit *our new nature can develop. It is gradual; Paul tells us it is a process... 'from one degree of glory to another'... Eventually when we see Christ, the change is complete. We will be in his likeness and the image of God restored! ...* This can be effected only by the work of the Holy Spirit in our lives. *(My emphasis)*[32]

Similarly, William Challis, in his excellent book on the role of the Bible in pastoral care, reminds us of the vital role of the Holy Spirit: 'When we use the Bible correctly in our pastoral work, when we acknowledge it as a vital pastoral resource, we discover that the Bible itself reminds us that it is the Holy Spirit who gives life to our pastoral theology and our pastoral work.'[33]

How, then, can we allow the Spirit to continue the work that God has begun? Let me suggest three ways from my own experience of pastoral ministry.

Firstly, we can pray, as Christian leaders, for ourselves to be filled with the Spirit. I knew that many of the pastoral situations I was facing in the course of my ministry were well beyond my scope.

This drove me to seek God for fresh power and anointing on my life and ministry: 'Lord, please fill my life again with fresh power and grace through your Spirit. I need you so much; I long for you to work through me! I come to the cross and surrender my life to you again.' The subsequent empowering would give me renewed energy and compassion to be alongside people in their pain and brokenness.

Secondly, we can ask the Holy Spirit to work powerfully and deeply in pastoral situations. I (and my prayer ministry and pastoral teams) wouldn't hesitate to pray with people after services, or in their homes, or in hospital or prison or the residential care home: 'Come, Lord Jesus, by your Spirit and meet your servant at their point of need today. Touch their life with your healing grace, restore the joy of their salvation, and fill them with a fresh experience of your love and power.' I am reminded of the powerful words of a well-loved song by David Evans, 'Be still':

Be still, for the power of the Lord
Is moving in this place;
He comes to cleanse and heal,
To minister his grace.
No work too hard for him,
In faith receive from him;
Be still, for the power of the Lord
Is moving in this place.[34]

Jim Packer, in his book Imperfect People, encourages us with the stories of biblical characters who were transformed by the power of God[35] and, in his article on the Holy Spirit in the *New Dictionary of Christian Ethics and Pastoral Theology*, says:

'Whatever problems of temperament, emotional scarring, past victimis-
ation, and present bad habits Christians may have, a vital element
of pastoral care is to hold before them the power of the Holy Spirit to
change the most unpromising human material into the moral likeness of

Jesus Christ, and to insist that the call to be transformed... may not be evaded.[36]

Thirdly, we can ask the Holy Spirit to give us wisdom and insight into particularly complex pastoral situations. At times in my ministry, it was very obvious what counsel to give, and sanctified common sense or some counselling training helped me enormously.[37] In other situations, the problem was not so apparent, and it was not clear what advice would be appropriate. So, as I listened carefully to people's painful stories, I would discipline myself to try to listen to the Holy Spirit as well, praying silently in the quietness of my own heart, 'Lord, what is this person's real need? What do you want to do in their life? Is there a particular word of challenge or encouragement for them, or a Bible verse that speaks directly into their situation?' It was only when I asked for this pastoral wisdom and insight that a word, picture or Bible verse would emerge. I never assumed that I had heard correctly from God, so I would always put it to them tentatively, giving them permission to reject it if it was not relevant: 'I don't know if this is helpful but some verses from Proverbs have come to mind. I think the Lord is asking you to trust him for the next step in your life, and he promises to direct your path. Does that make any sense to you at this time?'

CONCLUSION: WORD AND SPIRIT TOGETHER IN PASTORAL CARE AND NURTURE

Once again we see how God's Word and God's Spirit are our two greatest resources for ministry. In the particular area of pastoral care and nurture, we are incredibly blessed to have the Bible (which is full of pastoral wisdom) and the Spirit (who anoints us with power, wisdom and compassion). Armed with these two, we are able not only to be channels of God's blessing and grace into people's lives, but we can also be part of that ongoing process of transformation 'from one degree of glory to another'.[38] This links our pastoral ministry firmly into the core task of gospel ministry, as Paul wrote to the Philippians: 'Continue to work out your salvation with fear and trembling, for it is God who works in you to will and to act according to his good purpose.'[39]

Notes

1 This happened in 1974, when the initials 'IRA' were scratched across it.
2 Psalm 139:14
3 John 13:1–17
4 Luke 18:18–25; Matthew 23
5 Luke 11:20
6 Luke 4:18–19
7 Revelation 21:5
8 Derek Tidball, *Skilful Shepherds* (Apollos, 1997 edition)
9 Timothy Laniak, *Shepherds after My Own Heart* (Apollos, 2006)
10 Colossians 1:28; Ephesians 4:13
11 Ephesians 3:7; Colossians 1:23
12 John Stott, *The Contemporary Christian* (IVP, 1992), p. 290
13 John Hughes, *The Pastor's Notebook* (Kingsway, 2003), p. 247
14 Richard Baxter, *The Reformed Pastor* (Epworth Press reprint, 1939), pp. 121–122
15 Acts 13:1
16 1 Timothy 5:17; 1 Thessalonians 5:12; 1 Timothy 3:8; 4:14; 5:17; 2 Timothy 2:2
17 Wallace Benn, 'The Baxter model: guidelines for pastoring today', *Orthos* 13 (Fellowship of Word and Spirit, 1993), p. 9
18 Matthew 6:38–48; Luke 10:30–37; Matthew 25:31–46; 28:19–20
19 Romans 12:15
20 Galatians 6:2 (RSV)
21 John 15:12 (RSV)
22 1 John 3:16
23 Ephesians 4:12 (RSV)
24 Isaiah 40:1–2: 'Comfort, comfort my people, says your God. Speak tenderly to Jerusalem, and proclaim to her that her hard service has been completed.'
25 This is not to conclude that the Bible is only a pastoral document, because there were other reasons why it was written too (theological, evangelistic, apologetic, liturgical and discipleship reasons). The Bible has, however, real-life pastoral situations behind it that prompted the need to write, and it emphasises

not only the importance of good pastoral care but also the relevance of teaching the Bible in order to address parallel pastoral situations today.

26 Hebrews 4:12

27 Luke 4:18–19; based on Isaiah 61:1–2

28 Acts 1:8

29 See Colossians 1:28–29; 2 Corinthians 4:7–12; 12:9

30 Ephesians 1:13–14; Galatians 5:16–26; 2 Corinthians 3:17–18; Ephesians 4:14–16

31 Philippians 1:6

32 Roger Hurding, *Restoring the Image: An introduction to Christian caring and counselling* (Paternoster, 1980), pp. 10–11

33 William Challis, *The Word of Life: Using the Bible in pastoral care* (Marshall Pickering, 1997), p. 24

34 Extract taken from the song 'Be Still for the Presence of the Lord' by David J. Evans. Copyright © 1986 Thankyou Music*

35 Jim Packer, *Imperfect People: Never Beyond Hope* (Kingsway, 2000)

36 Jim Packer, 'The Holy Spirit', in David Atkinson and David Field (eds.), *New Dictionary of Christian Ethics and Pastoral Theology* (IVP, 1995), p. 447

37 For a helpful analysis of the relationship between pastoral care and counselling, see Roger Hurding's 'Pastoral Care, Counselling and Psychotherapy' in Atkinson and Field (eds.), *New Dictionary of Christian Ethics and Pastoral Theology*, Part 1, Chapter 12.

38 2 Corinthians 3:18 (RSV)

39 Philippians 2:12–13

MOTIVATING EVANGELISM
AND MISSION

I am writing this last chapter in the research library at the Church Mission Society headquarters in Oxford. It has 31,000 volumes and I am not going to pretend that I have read them all! What it has given me, though, as I have browsed the shelves, is an excitement at being part of an international family. From the initial commission given by Jesus to his disciples to preach the gospel to all nations,[1] the good news of Christ has gone out to the ends of the earth and Christianity has become a world faith, embracing nearly one-third of the world's population. We are enormously privileged to belong to an international community made up of 'every nation, tribe, people and language'.[2] Our Christian ministry in the harsh wastelands of the post-Christian Western world should be enriched and blessed by the vitality, wisdom and maturity of churches in other parts of the world, especially those that have experienced persecution as Christian minorities. This has certainly been my experience on regular trips to southern Uganda. Mission blossoms through partnership, and we desperately need our international family to help us, as they once needed us.

The CMS library has also impressed on me the importance of missiology. The task of mission is integral to our identity as the Church of Jesus Christ because we worship and serve a missionary God. There is a vast wealth of Christian writing on the subject and also a burgeoning range of studies in the area of 'mission-shaped church', 'fresh expressions of church' and 'emerging church'. All these books are examining crucial questions for the church in the West. What is the gospel and should our presentation of it change in different settings? How important is evangelism in the wider context of the church's total mission (including social compassion, social and global ethics, environmental care, Christian apologetics, Christianity in the workplace, Christianity in the arts and culture, and so on)? How does the gospel connect with different cultural contexts, and is all authentic Christian mission required to be incarnational? How might the gospel challenge the prevailing culture in any given context? How should Christianity relate to the other major world faiths and what is the place for interfaith dialogue and partnerships? How do we uphold the uniqueness of Christ in a pluralistic and relativist society, and yet continue to value human choice and religious freedom? In our post-Christian society in the West, should the mission strategy of historic denominations be to re-energise traditional churches, or create 'fresh expressions' of church, or have both existing side by side in a mixed economy? Is the focus of Christian mission to win converts and to make disciples (in other words, the growth of the church), or to transform society and enable it to reflect God's rule over the whole of life (the growth of the kingdom of God), or both?

Many of these questions are faced head-on in *Mission-Shaped Questions: Defining issues for today's church*,[3] and theological colleges are teaching in these areas with our emerging leaders. Yet anyone at the coalface of Christian ministry is living with these questions every day, and we cannot avoid them unless we are theological ostriches. Mission studies refuses to be sidelined as a minority interest for a few keen enthusiasts: the Church is the only society on earth that exists for the benefit of its non-members. The gospel created the Church, and the Church exists for the gospel.

Another striking impression from my week here in the library at CMS has been the way Christian mission is resourced by the Word and the Spirit. Numerous studies emphasise this point. For example, John Stott's *Christian Mission in the Modern World* argues that the preaching of the biblical gospel must be primary and central to all Christian mission, and he also appeals for a mission that is resourced by the power of the Spirit.[4] Lesslie Newbigin also stressed the partnership in his *Evangelism in the Context of Secularisation* (1990): he argued that the church must recover its confidence to use the Bible to explain who we really are, where we come from and where we are going, and yet this must be done in a Christian community that is being renewed by the Holy Spirit, so that it becomes the living hermeneutic for the gospel.[5] Likewise, *Salvation to the Ends of the Earth: A biblical theology of mission*, is written by two distinguished missiologists who want to ensure that contemporary patterns of mission and preaching of the gospel are directly rooted in the saving mission of Jesus as the Bible presents it, and that this is done 'in and through the power of the Holy Spirit'.[6]

Also, *A Time for Mission: The challenge for global Christianity*, written by Samuel Escobar, a seasoned evangelical missiologist, not only examines the insights of global Christianity but argues the case for a biblical theology of mission that sees the preaching of the gospel as central and the power of the Spirit as essential. He notes:

Great movements of missionary advance are born in the cradle of spiritual revival. When, by a special visitation of the Holy Spirit, Christians have a renewed sense of the majesty, the power and the love of God, the grace and compassion of Jesus Christ and the renewing fire of the Holy Spirit, the outcome is the renewal of missionary vocation... It is important to notice that during the twentieth century the strongest and most successful missionary action has come from the Pentecostal movement.[7]

Finally, by way of an example of the Word and Spirit partnership in mission, comes *The Road to Growth: Towards a thriving church* by Bob Jackson.[8] In his very important final chapter, entitled 'The road to growth through spiritual renewal', he comes up with a superb list of five suggestions that, he admits, are as old as the Church itself. One of them is the Bible: 'If the Bible is indeed "the word of the Lord" then hunger for its message will be at the heart of spiritual renewal.'[9] Another major source of renewal is what he calls 'spiritual encounter': 'Where genuine encounter with the living God is expected and experienced, congregations tend to grow... God made accessible in Christ by his Spirit through the Church, whatever the worship style, is the ultimate church growth draw.'[10]

All five of these studies encourage leaders to prioritise the ministries of both the Word and the Spirit in their obedience to the great commission.

MISSION-SHAPED CHURCHES NEED MISSION-SHAPED LEADERS

It is usually true that what flourishes in church life is directly related to what the church leader encourages, and what he/ she neglects will usually wither and die. Thankfully, there are wonderful exceptions to this rule. However, if it is normally true, then leaders cannot afford to take their eye off the ball here: we must be ever mindful of the calling on the church to 'declare the praises of him who called you out of darkness into his marvellous light'.[11] This is all the more important because, unlike places in the developing world where church growth is outstripping the population growth, fewer and fewer people overall are attending places of Christian worship in the West.[12] Callum Brown, in his book *The Death of Christian Britain*, writes, 'What is taking place is not only the continued decline of organised Christianity but the death of the culture that formerly conferred Christian identity on the British people as a whole. If a core identity survives for Britons, it is certainly no longer Christian. The culture of Christianity has gone in the Britain of the new Millennium.'[13] It is so important that we accept the death of Christendom, because, unless we do, we will never realise the size of the missionary task in front of us, and we will go on deceiving ourselves that people will eventually come back to the church. Gordon Bates, when Bishop of Whitby, wrote:

The Church has got to realise its missionary responsibilities. We live in a society, whether urban or rural, which is now basically second or even third generation pagan... Very many people have no residue of Christian faith at all; it's not just dormant, it's non-existent. In so many instances we have to go back to basics; we are in a critical missionary situation.[14]

Following the Church of England report *Mission-Shaped Church*, we re-examined all our church activities at St John's, Ealing, in the light of the great commission. We tried to ensure that our Sunday services were seeker-friendly in style and proclaimed the gospel. We were keen to maintain a Christian Basics course running con-secutively throughout the year, but also to tailor the course to other situations and people-group settings (such as young people, the elderly, people with English as a second language, and so on). We also created ways of ensuring that our community outreach groups, working with families or the elderly or the homeless, were helped to share the gospel. We tried to make sure that our home groups were equipping our church members for the task of mission, and we made church prayer meetings times of calling on God to fill us afresh with the power of the Holy Spirit. We put mission on the agenda of our church council and other church committees, and we budgeted for evangelism, as well as tithing our total church income to world mission. We wanted to be enriched by the vitality of global Christianity, so we took teams from the church to visit our mission partners in the developing world, as well as inviting developing world pastors to come over to us. All of this was expressed overtly in the mission dimension of our vision statement: 'At St John's we are called to... go out, in the power of the Spirit, to share the good news of Jesus in a broken world, to love and serve people in Ealing and beyond, to work for justice and to challenge oppression, and to live and work for his praise and glory.' In all of these ways we tried to ensure that mission was at the forefront of our life as a church, and we were hugely helped by God's two great resources for this task—his Word and his Spirit.

ALLOWING THE BIBLE TO MOTIVATE MISSION AND EVANGELISM

Firstly, all our preaching and teaching of the Bible should help our congregations to understand the task of mission that has been entrusted to them. Dr Chris Wright has written a magisterial work in which he has tried to unlock the Bible's 'grand narrative'. The title is, significantly, *The Mission of God*. His main point is clear: he establishes a biblical hermeneutic that 'sees the mission of God (and the participation in it of God's people) as a framework within which we can read the whole Bible'.[15] This means for us that every sermon (and every home group study and personal Bible study time, for that matter, too) should connect with the overarching mission of God at some point. What does this passage tell us about the gospel? What do we learn about God's amazing love in sending Jesus? How and why is Jesus the unique Saviour and Lord of the world? What do we learn about the responsibilities and tasks of Christian mission? In short, no part of the Bible is disconnected from God's mission plan. The preaching and teaching of the Bible are therefore central to our church's mission strategy.

Secondly, we must open the Bible and teach about Jesus in all our evangelism. The apostle John made this point clearly at the end of his gospel: 'These things are written that you may believe that Jesus is the Christ, the Son of God, and that by believing you may have life in his name.'[16] Luke illustrates the point in the story of the Ethiopian eunuch in Acts 8. The African court official is studying the book of Isaiah, trying to work out the identity of the suffering servant in chapter 53: 'Then Philip began with that very passage of Scripture and told him the good news about Jesus' (v. 35).

When I was a curate in Reigate, we invited the Revd Hugh Palmer (now Rector of All Souls, Langham Place, in London) to be our guest speaker for a mission week. I noticed that he used the Bible in every address, whether it was a Sunday guest service, dinner at the golf club, lunch for the pensioners, men's breakfast or women's coffee morning. His talks were not, therefore, his own bright ideas about Christianity, but a presentation of the real Jesus as the Bible presented him.

A similar thing happened more recently when we started our Café Church venture in Ealing, attracting 50–60 homeless people. For many weeks we worked our way through the Gospel of Mark, each evening containing first a talk illustrating the main points, followed by a small group discussion on the particular passage. Some of the group members needed help with their reading, and most had no background knowledge of the Bible, so everything had to be explained. Yet, as the weeks went by, they gradually grasped a picture of Jesus that surprised and thrilled them: one of the most telling comments was, 'I never knew that Jesus had time for people like us.' This is not to say that there isn't a place in evangelism for Christian apologetics (which itself is rooted in biblical theology), or Christian dramatic, musical or literary presentations, or testimonies, because all of them will (we hope) be presenting an aspect of gospel truth. But it is to highlight the essential requirement for any evangelistic endeavour: the Bible is opened, the biblical Jesus is presented, and there is a call on the hearers for repentance and faith.

Thirdly, for this to happen, we must help our congregations to have a working knowledge of the Bible for their own evangelism. This can happen, to a certain extent, through our preaching as we model the way a certain passage might be used to explain the gospel. At the same time, we need evangelism training days, when we talk through how we could help people to find Christ. I have used the story of Philip and the Ethiopian, in Acts 8:26–40, as a model for personal evangelism: Philip makes himself available for God to use him (8:4–6), he listens to the Spirit's prompting (vv. 26–29), he asks the right question (v. 30), he uses the Scriptures (vv. 32–35), he focuses on Christ (v. 35) and he leads his listener to a point of commitment (vv. 36–40). Beyond the methodology, we can help people to know which parts of the Bible are particularly useful for explaining the gospel: Isaiah 53; Luke 19:1–10; Acts 2:14–41; Romans 1—3; Ephesians 1:1–14 and so on. After all, as

Paul wrote to Timothy, the holy Scriptures were given to 'make you wise for salvation through faith in Jesus Christ'.[17]

ALLOWING THE SPIRIT TO EMPOWER AND EQUIP US

The Holy Spirit is our other great resource for Christian mission in at least four ways. Firstly, he orchestrates the Church's mission, by guiding each congregation to see their harvest field and to know which bits are 'ripe for harvest'.[18] Just as Paul and Barnabas were sent out from Antioch at the prompting of the Spirit,[19] so we should be expecting the Holy Spirit to prompt us to reach out to new areas and people groups. One striking example of this in my own experience was the way the Spirit called us to develop our ministry to the homeless in Ealing. The church had been feeding them at a soup kitchen every weekend for 30 years, but the Spirit challenged us to share the gospel with them, too, and to allow God to work deeply in their lives. The results were the appointment of a Christian homeless worker, the beginning of the Café Church ministry and the slow but steady healing of broken lives. Another example would be our growing sense that God was calling us to reach out to the neediest housing estates in our West Ealing parish. The Spirit was not only prompting us but also opening the door: 'Soul in the City' (London) brought a group of Christian teenagers to work with our church members in community outreach, and the impact of that fortnight had lasting effects for all the participating churches. Many committed themselves to an ongoing involvement on these housing estates, and it was wonderful to see lives changed and communities blessed. Both these initiatives were begun and continued under the Spirit's direction.

Secondly, the Spirit empowers the local church for the task of mission. I remember a sailing expedition on Derwent Water in the Lake District, when a family friend kindly offered to take us out in his small yacht. We were all ready to go, but there was one small problem: no wind! We had to sit tight and wait, and moved out of the marina only when a gentle breeze developed into a strong wind. The first disciples had to learn this lesson, and only after the mighty rushing wind of Pentecost[20] were they able to fulfil the great commission to take the gospel to the ends of the earth. We don't need to wait in exactly the same way, for the Spirit has now been sent upon the Church, but there is a prayerful dependency on the power of God that remains vital for all mission outreach.[21] All the revivals in Christian history were born in prayer, as we have seen.[22] In Bristol and in Ealing we learnt that prayer is still the power behind the Church's mission, and the Spirit's power comes when we call on his name.

Thirdly, the Spirit causes people to respond to the preaching of the gospel. We can't bring anyone to Christ, or open their eyes to understand the gospel, or give them the gift of faith, but the Spirit can. Indeed, this is his special work, so it is important that we have a healthy confidence and reliance on the Spirit as we reach out to our friends, neighbours and colleagues. I remember how, in the early days of starting the Alpha course in Ealing, we saw a number of non-Christian husbands come to faith. Their Christian wives had longed for this, but had not known how it could possibly happen. The Spirit's work through Alpha came as a joyful surprise.

Fourthly, the Spirit promotes the gospel through signs and wonders. In Acts 3, a crippled beggar is dramatically healed and restored, and this in turn leads to a wonderful opportunity to explain to the crowd how and why the healing had happened. The Spirit had been powerfully at work in the healing of this man, and was now using the opportunity for further gospel preaching. The same pattern recurs many times in Acts.[23] We have seen that there is every reason to trust that the gifts of the Spirit continue to be given to the Church in every generation,[24] so we should expect God to continue to work by his Spirit through signs and miracles, leading to opportunities for preaching and evangelism. In fact, not only do miracles often lead to evangelism, but evangelism sometimes leads to miracles.[25] While I don't think that the gospel needs any self-authentication, for it is itself the power of God for salvation,[26] and nor should we rely on miracles to attract attention, the biblical reality is that miracles do still happen, and they serve to advance the gospel. Such miracles are many and varied: they can involve physical or emotional healing, restoring of relationships or broken marriages, release from demon oppression or possession, or miraculous provision. I have personally witnessed all of these, and, in a movement like New Wine, they become normal and commonplace.

As leaders, we must be careful not to exclude or deny the Spirit's work, lest we become guilty of grieving him. There is an old story about Thomas Aquinas when he was summoned by the Pope to come to Rome. The pontiff showed him the glory of Rome and said, 'Look, Thomas, we can no longer say, "Silver and gold have I none."' Thomas replied, 'Yes, your holiness, but neither can we say, "Rise up and walk."'[27]

CONCLUSION

The Edinburgh 2010 World Missionary Conference took place in June 2010 to commemorate the 100th anniversary of the famous mission conference held in the Scottish capital in 1910. Leaders of the ecumenical and Evangelical movements reaffirmed their commitment to witnessing to Christ. Dr Geoff Tunnicliffe, the international director of the World Evangelical Alliance, addressed some 300 leaders from across the Christian denominations and traditions, and drew attention to the conference's theme, 'Witnessing to Christ today'. He said:

We are not talking about some vaguely theistic or humanist agenda, but bearing glad witness to Jesus Christ, the second person of the Trinity... There is no authentic Christian mission that does not bear witness to him in word and deed and character, both individually and corporately. And there is no authentic church that does not have a passionate commitment to mission, reflecting the heart of Father, Son and Holy Spirit.[28]

He then emphasised that authentic Christian mission was a partnership of Word and Spirit:

God's calling to the whole church is to take the whole gospel to the whole world, and that call comes anew to us in every generation… I hope that in these few days we will ponder that, with humility and repentance, and with renewed commitment to bear witness to Christ, with the love of the Father and in the power of the Holy Spirit, in every corner of the globe.[29]

Similarly, in his final speech of the recent Lausanne Congress for World Evangelisation in Cape Town, South Africa (October 2010), the International Director of Lausanne, Lindsay Brown, emphasised the need to allow the Spirit to transform our lives as we proclaim the gospel to a watching world: 'The word of truth has to be backed up by authentic, transformed, joyful lives.'[30] Likewise, at the end of my leadership lecture on 'Motivating mission and evangelism', I leave my students with two short exhortations: 'Preach the gospel!'[31] and 'Pray for power!'[32] I tell them that those are Jesus' commands, not mine. Can you imagine the impact on their future parishes, the nation and the world if they did that faithfully throughout their 30 or 40 years in ministry?

Notes

1   Matthew 28:18–20
2   Revelation 7:9
3   Steven Croft, *Mission-Shaped Questions* (CHP, 2008)
4   John Stott, *Christian Mission in the Modern World* (Falcon, 2nd edn 1977), pp. 124–127
5   Paul Weston (ed.), *Lesslie Newbigin, Missionary Theologian: A reader* (SPCK, 2006), pp. 232–234
6   A. Kostenberger and P. O'Brien, *Salvation to the Ends of the Earth: A biblical theology of mission*, New Studies in Biblical Theology (IVP, 2001), p. 128
7   Samuel Escobar, *A Time for Mission: The challenge for global Christianity* (Langham Partnership International/IVP, 2003), p. 94

8   He was the Archdeacon of Walsall and Growth Officer for the Lichfield Diocese, but previously he was an economist, a parish priest and then a member of Springboard, the Archbishop of Canterbury's initiative to encourage, renew and mobilise the church for evangelism.

9   Bob Jackson, *The Road to Growth: Towards a thriving church* (CHP, 2nd impression 2008), p. 221

10 Jackson, *Road to Growth*, p. 225

11 1 Peter 2:9

12 Jackson, *Road to Growth*, p. 5

13 Callum Brown, *The Death of Christian Britain* (Routledge, 2000), pp. 193, 198

14 The Rt Revd Gordon Bates, *Church Army News*, April 1998

15 Christopher Wright, *The Mission of God: Unlocking the Bible's grand narrative* (IVP, 2006), p. 17

16 John 20:31

17 2 Timothy 3:15

18 John 4:35

19 Acts 13:2

20 Acts 2:2 (RSV)

21 Acts 1:8

22 See pages 143–145.

23 For example, Acts 5:12–16; 6:8–10; 13:6–12

24 See pages 122–126.

25 For example, Acts 8:9–13; 14:8–10; 19:8–12

26 Romans 1:16

27 For a much fuller discussion of the place of signs and wonders in evangelism, see John Wimber, *Power Evangelism* (Hodder, 1985), Don Williams, *Signs, Wonders and the Kingdom of God* (1989) or Derek Morphew, *Breakthrough* (Vineyard International, 1991).

28 See www.edinburgh2010.org/en/resources/papersdocuments.html

29 See www.edinburgh2010.org/en/resources/papersdocuments.html

30 http://conversation.lausanne.org/en

31 Matthew 28:19–20; Mark 16:15

32 Luke 24:48–49; Acts 1:14

✣

CONCLUSION: THE COURAGE TO EMBRACE BOTH

Imagine what it must have been like to be the prophet Ezekiel. The hand of the Lord is upon him, and God leads him into the middle of a valley, full of dry bones (Ezekiel 37:1–14). The sight of such devastation overwhelms him and he wishes he could run away. God then explains that he wants to use Ezekiel to bring these bones back to life, for he is going to restore his people after their exile in Babylon. For this to happen, the prophet will need to do two things: he must speak the Word of the Lord to these dead people (v. 4), and he must call on the breath of God's Spirit to come and give new life (v. 9). If just being there was uncomfortable enough for the prophet, having to be God's chosen person to turn the situation around must have been absolutely terrifying. It required tremendous courage to embrace the ministry of Word and Spirit, so that God's purposes could be fulfilled at this crucial stage in Israel's history.

In a similar way, great courage is required of Christian leaders as we face the spiritual exile of post-Christendom and the spiritual wastelands of postmodernity. Being there is hard enough, but we too are called to be God's people and embrace the ministries of Word and Spirit. This is how God accomplishes his eternal purposes for his world; this is how dry bones are brought back to life. This is how God restores his people and extends his kingdom.

The central thesis of this book is that gospel ministry is resourced by the vital partnership—the Word of God and the Spirit of God. While some churches emphasise a 'ministry of the Word' and others emphasise a 'ministry of the Spirit', I have argued that Jesus always intended that we allow for both, and we are meant to be blessed by both. This is true to the emphasis of the Bible, consistent with our Christian history and evangelical heritage, and vital for the healthy growth of our churches today. The Church is *both* a community gathered round and sent out by the Word of God *and* a community indwelt and empowered by the Spirit of God. Our leadership, therefore, must reflect these two glorious truths.

To be a Word and Spirit person means to sit humbly under the authority of the Bible, to study it, obey it and preach it. We must give ourselves to this task with unswerving devotion and patience, for it is an exhausting and exacting ministry that will demand our best efforts. So many leaders have given up on biblical exposition for this very reason: it is much easier to throw together a few spiritual platitudes, loosely connected to a Bible passage, than to get down to the hard graft of studying (and praying over) the passage, reading the commentaries, and explaining and applying the meaning, lovingly and pastorally, to our people. Alongside this, we are entirely dependent on the ministry of God's Spirit, giving us wisdom and insight, strengthening us with power and grace, equipping us with spiritual gifts and transforming us and our people into the likeness of Christ. It will require a daily openness to the Spirit's work, resting under his sovereignty, being reassured of the Father's love, being restored with God's mercy and forgiveness, being renewed in our hearts with love and devotion to Christ, and being refilled with power and strength for service.

Does it matter? Maybe we are still not convinced about this vital partnership in the practice of our Christian leadership. Perhaps we are fearful of doing something that is unbiblical (which is a good thing to fear, so we need to go back and re-examine the biblical evidence), perhaps we are anxious about our Christian peer group and what they might think (which is *not* always a good thing, especially if God is calling us to make a change) and perhaps we are hesitating because we are comfortable as we are and change is always unsettling (which is not a good reason for *not* making a change).

Is there one decisive reason? For me, the decisive factor is

Christological. As we have seen, both Word and Spirit have ministries that point away from themselves to Christ. Both have 'floodlight ministries' that exalt and honour Jesus. Both equip the Church to present Christ faithfully to the world, and both ensure that Christ's saving purposes are accomplished. So, to embrace a full-bodied ministry of the Word and the Spirit is to be concerned for the honour and glory of Christ. There is no better reason.

✛

FOR FURTHER READING

1. THE CURRENT NEED FOR A CLOSER PARTNERSHIP

Gospel and Spirit, published by the Fountain Trust and the Church of England Council (The Abbey Press, April 1977)

Jim Packer, *Keep in Step with the Spirit* (IVP, 1984)

Donald Bridge, *Power Evangelism and the Word of God* (Kingsway, 1987)

Donald Bloesch, *A Theology of Word and Spirit* (IVP, 1992)

David Pawson, *Word and Spirit Together* (Hodder and Stoughton, 1998)

Rich Nathan and Ken Wilson, *Empowered Evangelicals* (Vine Books, 1997)

Larry Hart, *Truth Aflame* (Thomas Nelson, 1999)

Simon Ponsonby, *God Inside Out* (Kingsway, 2007)

Patrick Johnstone, *Operation World* (OM Publishing, 1996 edition)

John Stott, *Evangelical Truth* (IVP, 1999)

Rob Warner, *Reinventing English Evangelicalism 1966–2001* (Paternoster, 2007)

John Stott, *The Living Church* (IVP, 2007)

Douglas Groothius, *Truth Decay* (IVP, 2000)

Gerard Kelly, *Get a Grip on the Future* (Monarch, 1999)

Graham Cray, *Postmodern Culture and Youth Discipleship* (Grove, reprinted 2000)

Robert Webber, *The Younger Evangelicals* (Baker, 2002)

Roger Steer, *Church on Fire* (Hodder, 1998)

Shaping the Future: New patterns of training for lay and ordained (Ministry Division, CHP, 2006)

Common Worship: The ordination of Priests and Deacons (CHP, 2000)

2. BIBLICAL PERSPECTIVES

D.A. Carson, R.T. France and J.A. Motyer, *New Bible Commentary* (IVP, 2005 reprint)

J. Rodman Williams, *Renewal Theology* (Zondervan, 1996)

Wayne Grudem, *Systematic Theology* (IVP, 1994)

Vaughan Roberts, *God's Big Picture* (IVP, 2003)

Graeme Goldsworthy, *Gospel and Kingdom* (Paternoster, 1981)

John Stott, *Understanding the Bible* (SU, revised 1984)

W.H. Griffith Thomas, *The Holy Spirit of God* (Church Room Press, 1974)

Gordon Fee, *God's Empowering Presence* (Hendrickson, 1994)

James Robson, *Word and Spirit in Ezekiel* (Library of Hebrew Bible/ Old Testament Studies, T&T Clark, 2006)

John Stott, *Calling Christian Leaders* (IVP, 2002)

3. HISTORICAL PERSPECTIVES

Jonathan Hill, *The New Lion History of Christianity* (Lion Hudson, 2007)

Stephen Neill, *A History of Christian Missions* (Penguin, 1984 edition)

Clyde E. Fant and William M. Pinson (eds.), *Twenty Centuries of Great Preaching* (Word, 1976)

Simon Ponsonby, *God Inside Out* (Kingsway, 2007)

Ronald Kydd, *Charismatic Gifts in the Early Church* (Hendrickson, 1984)

Tim Dowley (ed.), *The Monarch History of the Church* Vols 1–5 (Monarch, 2005)

Owen Chadwick (ed.), *The Pelican History of the Church* Vols 1–5 (Penguin, 1960)

Alister McGrath, *An Introduction to Christianity* (Blackwell, 1997)

Gary Badcock, *Light of Truth and Fire of Love* (Eerdmans, 1997)

Stanley Burgess, *The New International Dictionary of Pentecostal and Charismatic Movements* (Zondervan, 2003)

Michael Mitton, *Restoring the Woven Cord: Strands of Celtic Christianity for the Church today* (BRF, 2010)

Brian Gaybba, *The Spirit of Love* (Geoffrey Chapman, 1987)

Water Elwell (ed.), *Evangelical Dictionary of Theology* (Marshall Pickering, 1984)

Geoffrey Nuttall, *The Holy Spirit in Puritan Faith and Experience* (Chicago, 1992)

E. Towns and D. Porter, *The Ten Greatest Revivals Ever* (Vine, 2000)

Jack Deere, *Surprised by the Voice of God* (Kingsway, 1996)

Geoffrey Hanks, *Seventy Great Christians* (Christian Focus, 1992)

David Bebbington, *Evangelicalism in Modern Britain* (Unwin Hyman, 1989)

David Watson, *I Believe in the Church* (Hodder and Stoughton, 1978)

David Watson, *You Are My God* (Hodder and Stoughton, 1983)

Michael Green, *I Believe in the Holy Spirit* (Hodder and Stoughton, 1975)

4. PREACHING AND TEACHING THE BIBLE

Chris Ash, *The Priority of Preaching* (Christian Focus/Proclamation Trust Media, 2009)

Greg Haslam (ed.), *Preach the Word!* (Sovereign World, 2006)

John Stott, *I Believe in Preaching* (Hodder, 1982)

Michael Quicke, *360-Degree Leadership: Preaching to transform congregations* (Baker, 2006)

Martin Lloyd-Jones, *Preaching and Preachers* (Hodder, 1971)

Chris Green and David Jackman (eds.), *When God's Voice Is Heard* (IVP, 1995)

Mark Stibbe, *The Teacher's Notebook* (Kingsway, 2003)

John Stott, *The Contemporary Christian* (IVP, 1992)

Rosie Ward, *Growing Women Leaders* (BRF, 2008)

R.T. Kendal, *The Anointing* (Hodder, 1998)

John Piper, *The Supremacy of God in Preaching* (IVP, 1990)

5. DEVELOPING AND IMPLEMENTING VISION

Bill Hybels, *Courageous Leadership* (Zondervan, 2002)

John Stott, *The Living Church* (IVP, 2007)

James Lawrence, *Growing Leaders* (BRF, 2004)

Rick Warren, *The Purpose Driven Church* (Zondervan, 1995)

Zachary Veron, *Leadership on the Front Foot* (Anglican Press Australia, 2009)

John Maxwell, *The 360-Degree Leader* (Thomas Nelson, 2005)

Greg Ogden and Daniel Meyer, *Leadership Essentials: Shaping vision, multiplying influence, defining character* (IVP Connect, 2007)

6. WORKING IN TEAMS AND MENTORING LEADERS

Aubrey Malphurs and Will Mancini, *Building Leaders* (Baker, 2004)

Bill Hybels, *Courageous Leadership* (Zondervan, 2002)

James Lawrence, *Growing Leaders* (BRF, 2004)

Rick Warren, *The Purpose Driven Church* (Zondervan, 1995)

John Eddison (ed.), *Bash: A study in spiritual power* (Marshall, 1983)

John Stott, *Guard the Gospel* (IVP, 1973)

David Watson, *You Are My God* (Hodder, 1983)

7. MOBILISING EVERY MEMBER INTO MINISTRY

David Watson, *I Believe in the Church* (Hodder, 1978)

John Stott, *The Living Church* (IVP, 2007)

John Stott, *God's New Society* (IVP, 1979)

Jack Deere, *Surprised by the Power of the Spirit* (Kingsway, 1993)

Max Turner, *The Holy Spirit and Spiritual Gifts* (Hendrickson, 1996)

Rick Warren, *The Purpose Driven Church* (Zondervan, 1995)

Tim Chester, *Total Church: A radical re-shaping around gospel and community* (Crossway, 2008)

Colin Martyn and Tony Payne, *The Trellis and the Vine* (Matthias Media, 2009)

8. ENABLING WORSHIP AND PRAYER

John Leech, *Living Liturgy* (Kingsway, 1997)

Michael Sadgrove, *Wisdom and Ministry: The call to leadership* (SPCK, 2008)

Christopher Cocksworth and Rosalind Brown, *Being a Priest Today* (Canterbury Press, 2nd edition 2006)

John Pritchard, *The Life and Work of a Priest* (SPCK, 2007)

John Stott, *Issues Facing Christians Today* (Zondervan, 4th edition revised 2006)

Jonathan Lamb, *Integrity: Leading with God watching* (IVP, 2006)

Simon Ponsonby, *More: How you can have more of the Spirit when you have everything in Christ* (Victor, 2004)

John Piper, *Desiring God: The pathway to spiritual growth* (Hodder, 2008 edition)

Charlie Cleverly, *The Discipline of Intimacy* (Kingsway, 2002)

Nicky Gumbel, *The Heart of Revival* (Kingsway, 1997)

Philip Yancey, *Prayer: Does it make any difference?* (Hodder, 2006)

Richard Foster, *Celebration of Discipline: The pathway to spiritual growth* (Hodder, 2008 edition)

Richard Foster, *Streams of Living Water: Celebrating the great traditions of the Christian faith* (HarperCollins, 1999)

Michael Green, *On Your Knees! St Paul at prayer* (Eagle, 1992)

9. PROVIDING PASTORAL CARE AND NURTURE

David Atkinson and David Field (eds.), *New Dictionary of Christian Ethics and Pastoral Theology* (IVP, 1995)

Derek Tidball, *Skilful Shepherds* (Apollos, 1997 edition)

Timothy Laniak, *Shepherds After My Own Heart* (Apollos, 2006)

Jim Packer, *Imperfect People: Never beyond hope* (Kingsway, 2000)

John Stott, *The Contemporary Christian* (IVP, 1992)

John Hughes, *The Pastor's Notebook* (Kingsway, 2003)

William Challis, *The Word of Life: Using the Bible in pastoral care* (Marshall Pickering, 1997)

Richard Baxter, *The Reformed Pastor* (Epworth Press, 1939)

Wallace Benn, 'The Baxter model: guidelines for pastoring today', *Orthos* 13 (Fellowship of Word and Spirit, 1993)

Roger Hurding, *Restoring the Image: An introduction to Christian caring and counselling* (Paternoster, 1980)

10. MOTIVATING EVANGELISM AND MISSION

Campbell Campbell-Jack and Gavin McGrath (eds.), *New Dictionary of Christian Apologetics* (IVP, 2006)

Steven Croft, *Mission-Shaped Questions* (CHP, 2008)

John Stott, *Christian Mission in the Modern World* (Falcon, 2nd edition 1977)

Paul Weston (ed.), *Lesslie Newbigin, Missionary Theologian: A reader* (SPCK, 2006)

Andrew Walls and Cathy Ross, *Mission in the 21st Century: Exploring the five marks of global mission* (Orbis, 2008)

A. Köstenberger and P. O'Brien, *Salvation to the Ends of the Earth: A biblical theology of mission*, New Studies in Biblical Theology (IVP, 2001)

Samuel Escobar, *A Time for Mission: The challenge for global Christianity* (Langham Partnership International and IVP, 2003)

Bob Jackson, *The Road to Growth: Towards a thriving church* (CHP, 2nd impression 2008)

Callum Brown, *The Death of Christian Britain* (Routledge, 2000)

Christopher Wright, *The Mission of God: Unlocking the Bible's grand narrative* (IVP, 2006)

John Wimber, *Power Evangelism* (Hodder, 1985)

Don Williams, *Signs, Wonders and the Kingdom of God* (Servant, 1989)

Derek Morphew, *Breakthrough* (Vineyard International, 1991)

Robin Gamble, *Jesus the Evangelist* (David Cook, 2009)

Michael Moynagh, *emergingchurch.intro* (Monarch, 2005)

Michael Green, *Evangelism through the Local Church* (Hodder and Stoughton, 1990)

Don Carson, *Telling the Truth: Evangelising postmoderns* (Zondervan, 2002)

J. John, *Breaking the News* (Authentic, 2009)

cpas

CPAS is an Anglican evangelical mission agency working with churches, mainly in the UK and the Republic of Ireland. Its tools, training and resources enable churches to help every person hear and discover the good news of Jesus Christ.

To find out more about the ministry of CPAS, please visit www.cpas.org.uk.

CPAS
Athena Drive
Tachbrook Park
WARWICK
CV34 6NG

Tel: 01926 458458
Email: info@cpas.org.uk

This book is dedicated to my wonderful wife, Ruth,
who has been my constant friend and partner in ministry,
and to my four amazing children, James, Ellie, Katherine and Ben,
who have journeyed with us and been such a blessing.